Easy
Beading

Vol. 6

Fast. Fashionable. Fun.

The best projects from the sixth year of *BeadStyle* magazine

KALMBACH BOOKS

Kalmbach Books
21027 Crossroads Circle
Waukesha, Wisconsin 53186
www.Kalmbach.com/books

Published in 2010

14 13 12 11 10   1 2 3 4 5

Printed in China

ISBN: 978-0-87116-291-5

All projects have appeared previously in *BeadStyle* magazine. *BeadStyle* is a registered trademark.

Publisher's Cataloging-In-Publication Data

Easy beading. Vol. 6 : fast, fashionable, fun : the best projects from the sixth
   year of BeadStyle magazine.

   p., : col. ill. ; cm.

   All projects have appeared previously in BeadStyle magazine.
   Includes index.
   ISBN: 978-0-87116-291-5

1. Beadwork--Handbooks, manuals, etc. 2. Beads--Handbooks, manuals, etc.
3. Jewelry making--Handbooks, manuals, etc. I. Title: BeadStyle Magazine.

TT860 .E27 2010
745.594/2

Contents

53

76

19

90 Metal and chain

92

138 Mixed media

177

204

230

Introduction

Recently, when my mom was looking through the latest issue of *BeadStyle,* she remarked to me that "we make it look so easy."

She is not a beader, so the world of *BeadStyle* is kind of a mystery to her. The truth is, though, with the proper tools (and a little practice), beading is easy.

Of course, "tools" are more than just pliers and wire cutters. Inspiration is the most important tool, but you also need to have some go-to techniques to make your ideas a reality. And you need to know what kinds of materials will realize your vision.

This sixth volume of *Easy Beading* — like the ones that came before — gives you all these essentials.

On the following pages, you'll find the step-by-step instructions for all the techniques you'll need to make beautiful jewelry. You'll also find a great visual bead glossary to give you some guidance when shopping for beads. And probably most importantly, you'll find the inspiration to create gorgeous jewelry that really expresses your creativity and style.

As in previous volumes, we've organized the inspiration of *Easy Beading* by materials used: gemstones, crystals, metal and chain, mixed media, pearls, and glass and ceramic. Check your local bead store and craft store first for supplies. We've provided specific information for unique items for your convenience.

Easy Beading includes projects for a range of skill levels. After all, even if you've mastered the basic techniques and can tell a briolette from a teardrop, you can never get enough inspiration.

If you are a beginner, congratulations! You've found the perfect book. In a just a couple of hours or less, you can make a beautiful, stylish piece of jewelry that's all about you. I hope you find these projects as inspiring as we did.

Warmest regards,

Cathy

CATHY JAKICIC,
EDITOR, *BEADSTYLE* **MAGAZINE**
editor@beadstylemag.com

Beader's Glossary

A visual reference to common beads and findings

gemstone shapes

lentil

rondelle

faceted
rondelle

round

oval

marquise

rectangle

tube

briolette

teardrop

chips

nugget

crystal and glass

Czech fire-polished

bicone

top-drilled bicone

cube

oval

drop

briolette

cone

round

saucer

top-drilled saucer
(with jump ring)

flat back

dichroic

lampworked

glass flowers

leaves

dagger

teardrop

fringe drops

seed beads

triangle

cube

bugle

pearls, shells, and miscellaneous

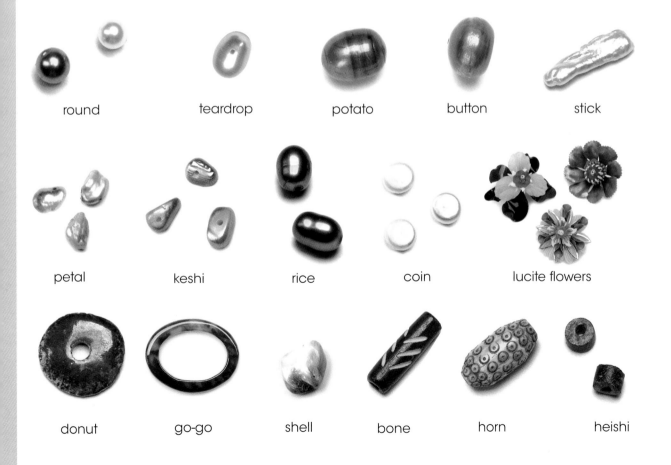

round

teardrop

potato

button

stick

petal

keshi

rice

coin

lucite flowers

donut

go-go

shell

bone

horn

heishi

findings, spacers, and connectors

French hook
ear wires

post earring
finding

hoop earring

lever-back
earring finding

ear
thread

magnetic
clasp

S-hook
clasp

lobster claw
clasp

toggle
clasp

two-strand
toggle clasp

box
clasp

slide
clasp

hook-and-eye
clasps

snap
clasp

pinch crimp
end

crimp
ends

coil end

crimp cone

tube bail
with loop

tube-shaped
and round crimp
beads

crimp
covers

bead tips

jump rings and
soldered jump
rings

split ring

spacers

bead
caps

pinch bail

multistrand
spacer bars

two-strand
curved tube

single-strand
tube

3-to-1 and 2-to-1
connectors

5-to-1 chandelier
component

bail

cone

tools, stringing materials, and chain

crimping pliers

chainnose pliers

roundnose pliers

bentnose pliers

split-ring pliers

diagonal wire
cutters

heavy-duty
wire cutters

ring
mandrel

twisted wire
beading needle

decorative head pin,
head pin, eye pin

sterling silver wire

memory wire

colored craft
wire

leather cord

suede cord

waxed
linen

beading
thread

flexible beading
wire

curb chain

rolo chain

long-and-short chain

figaro chain

cable chain

Basics
A step-by-step reference to key jewelry-making techniques used in bead-stringing projects.

plain loop

1 Trim the wire or head pin ⅜ in. (1 cm) above the top bead. Make a right angle bend close to the bead.

2 Grab the wire's tip with round-nose pliers. The tip of the wire should be flush with the pliers. Roll the wire to form a half circle. Release the wire.

3 Reposition the pliers in the loop and continue rolling.

4 The finished loop should form a centered circle above the bead.

wrapped loop

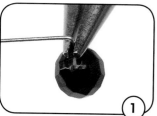

1 Make sure you have at least 1¼ in. (3.2 cm) of wire above the bead. With the tip of your chainnose pliers, grasp the wire directly above the bead. Bend the wire (above the pliers) into a right angle.

2 Using roundnose pliers, position the jaws in the bend as shown.

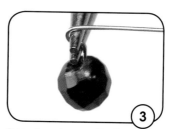

3 Bring the wire over the top jaw of the roundnose pliers.

4 Reposition the pliers' lower jaw snugly into the loop. Curve the wire downward around the bottom of the roundnose pliers. This is the first half of a wrapped loop.

5 To make the second half of the wrapped loop, position the chainnose pliers' jaws across the loop.

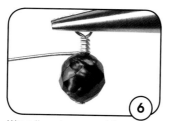

6 Wrap the wire around the wire stem, covering the stem between the loop and the top bead. Trim the excess wire and press the cut end close to the wraps with chainnose pliers.

opening and closing loops or jump rings

1 Hold the loop or jump ring with two pairs of chainnose pliers or chainnose and roundnose pliers, as shown.

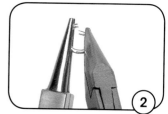

2 To open the loop or jump ring, bring one pair of pliers toward you and push the other pair away. Reverse the steps to close the open loop or jump ring.

Opening a split ring

To open a split ring, slide the hooked tip of split-ring pliers between the two overlapping wires.

surgeon's knot

Cross the right end over the left end and go through the loop. Go through again. Pull the ends to tighten. Cross the left end over the right end and go through once. Pull the ends to tighten.

overhand knot

Make a loop and pass the working end through it. Pull the ends to tighten the knot.

lark's head knot

Fold a cord in half and lay it behind a ring, loop, etc. with the fold pointing down. Bring the ends through the ring from back to front, then through the fold and tighten.

making wraps above a top-drilled bead

Center a top-drilled bead on a 3-in. (7.6 cm) piece of wire. Bend each wire upward to form a squared-off U shape.

Cross the wires into an X above the bead.

Using chainnose pliers, make a small bend in each wire so they form a right angle.

Wrap the horizontal wire around the vertical wire as in a wrapped loop. Trim the excess wrapping wire.

folded crimp end

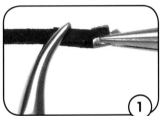

Glue one end of the cord and place it in a crimp end. Use chainnose pliers to fold one side of the crimp end over the cord.

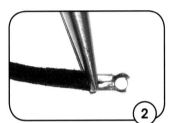

Repeat on the second side and squeeze gently. Test to be sure the crimp end is secure.

flat crimp

Hold the crimp using the tip of your chainnose pliers. Squeeze the pliers firmly to flatten the crimp.

Tug the wire to make sure the crimp has a solid grip. If the wire slides, repeat the steps with a new crimp.

folded crimp

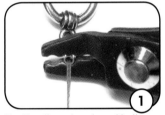

Position the crimp bead in the notch closest to the crimping pliers' handle.

Separate the wires and firmly squeeze the crimp.

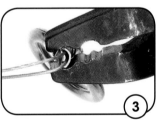

Move the crimp into the notch at the pliers' tip and hold the crimp as shown. Squeeze the crimp bead, folding it in half at the indentation.

Test that the folded crimp is secure.

cutting flexible beading wire

Decide how long you want your necklace to be. Add 6 in. (15 cm) and cut a piece of beading wire to that length. (For a bracelet, add 5 in./13 cm.)

Gemstones

Graduating
made easy

A strand of diamond-shaped
beads yields a striking
necklace and earrings

by Rupa Balachandar

When you start with a strand of graduated beads, it's easy to make a necklace by simply alternating the largest beads with metal ones. The greater the difference in size among the graduated beads, the more dramatic the resulting necklace will be. Save the smallest beads for a pair of earrings.

1 necklace • Cut a piece of beading wire (Basics, p. 12). Center the largest diamond-shaped bead. On each end, string a metal accent bead.

2 On each end, string the next largest diamond, an accent bead, the next largest diamond, and an accent bead.

3 On each end, alternate four to six successively smaller diamonds with 3 mm round spacers. Repeat, substituting 2 mm round spacers.

4 On each end, string four successively smaller diamonds.

5 On each end, string: flat spacer, crimp bead, 2 mm spacer, Wire Guardian, half of a clasp. Check the fit, and add or remove beads from each end if necessary. Go back through the beads just strung and tighten the wire. Crimp the crimp bead (Basics) and trim the excess wire.

Tip

Instead of cutting the strand of graduated beads on one end, cut it in the center. That way, it will be easier to string the beads in a graduated pattern.

Supplies

necklace 22 in. (56 cm)
- 16-in. (41 cm) strand 7–38 mm graduated diamond-shaped beads
- **6** 10 mm metal accent beads
- **2** 3 mm flat spacers
- **8–12** 3 mm round spacers
- **10–14** 2 mm round spacers
- flexible beading wire, .014 or .015
- **2** crimp beads
- **2** Wire Guardians
- toggle clasp

- chainnose or crimping pliers
- diagonal wire cutters

earrings
- **4** 7–12 mm diamond-shaped beads
- **2** 2–3 mm round spacers
- **2** 1½-in. (3.8 cm) head pins
- pair of earring wires
- chainnose and roundnose pliers
- diagonal wire cutters

1 earrings • On a head pin, string a diamond-shaped bead, a spacer, and a diamond. Make a plain loop (Basics, p. 12).

Design alternative

Try a different bead shape: String a version with graduated ruby jade rondelles and copper findings.

2 Open the loop of an earring wire (Basics) and attach the dangle. Close the loop. Make a second earring to match the first.

The long leafy link is anchored by the faceted teardrop pendant.

String fresh spring green

An easy pattern gives way to a gorgeous necklace and earrings

by Jennifer Gorski

Green amethyst is often mistaken for other gemstones, like peridot and tourmaline. It is sold under a variety of names, such as vermarine, green quartz, lime citrine, or prasiolite. To play up its pale yellow color, choose silver accents.

1 necklace • Open a jump ring (Basics, p. 12) and attach a pendant and a loop of a metal link. Close the jump ring. Attach another jump ring to the link's other loop.

2 Cut a piece of beading wire (Basics) and center the pendant.

3 On each end, string: bicone crystal, coin, bicone, bead cap, 12 mm pearl, bead cap. Repeat three times.

4 On each end, string a bicone, a 6 mm pearl, a bicone, and a 6 mm. String bicones until the strand is within 1½ in. (3.8 cm) of the finished length.

5 On one end, string a crimp bead, a bicone, and a lobster claw clasp. Repeat on the other end, substituting a 1½-in. (3.8 cm) piece of chain for the clasp. Check the fit, and add or remove beads if necessary. Go back through the last few beads strung and tighten the wire.

6 Crimp the crimp beads (Basics) and trim the excess wire. Close a crimp cover over each crimp. On a head pin, string a bead. Make the first half of a wrapped loop (Basics). Attach the end link of the chain and complete the wraps.

❝I don't force the creative process. When I'm not in 'the place,' I leave it alone until a new idea comes to me.❞

1 earrings • On a head pin, string: bicone crystal, coin, bead cap, bicone. Make a wrapped loop (Basics, p. 12).

2 Open an earring wire's loop (Basics). Attach the dangle and close the loop. Make a second earring to match the first.

Supplies

necklace 18½ in. (47 cm)
- 20 mm teardrop-shaped pendant
- **8** 13 mm faceted gemstone coins
- **8** 12 mm glass pearls
- **4** 6 mm glass pearls
- **24–34** 4 mm bicone crystals
- 35 mm metal link with two loops (You And Me Findings, youandmefindings.net)
- **16** 9 mm bead caps
- flexible beading wire, .014 or .015
- 2-in. (5 cm) head pin
- **2** 4 mm jump rings
- **2** crimp beads
- **2** crimp covers
- lobster claw clasp
- 1½ in. (3.8 cm) chain for extender, 7–8 mm links
- chainnose and roundnose pliers, or **2** pairs of chainnose pliers
- diagonal wire cutters
- crimping pliers (optional)

earrings
- **2** 13 mm faceted gemstone coins
- **4** 4 mm bicone crystals
- **2** 9 mm bead caps
- **2** 2-in. (5 cm) head pins
- pair of lever-back earring wires
- chainnose and roundnose pliers
- diagonal wire cutters

Design alternative

When you're in the mood for just a wee bit o' green, a CZ pendant attached to a metal link and hung from chain is a quick option.

Tip

For the earrings, use your chainnose pliers to carefully bend the bead caps to fit around the coins.

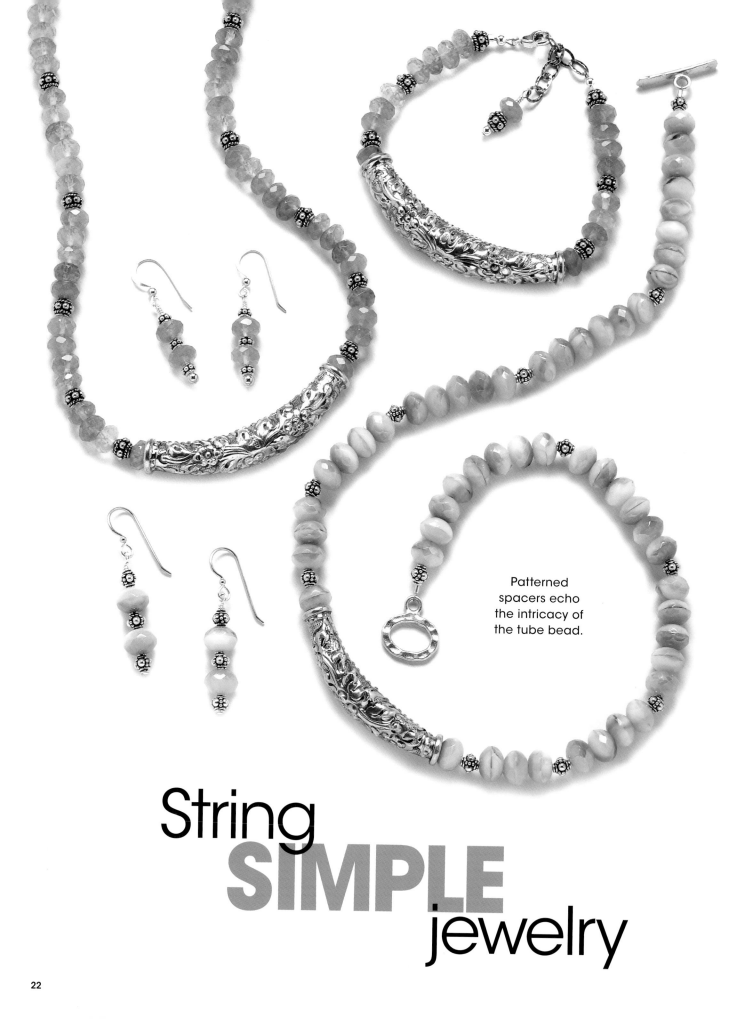

Patterned spacers echo the intricacy of the tube bead.

String SIMPLE jewelry

Make an easy necklace, bracelet, and earrings in less than 30 minutes

by Laurie Feldman

Give new meaning to quicksilver: Combine a curved silver tube bead with faceted rondelles in shades of cool mint or juicy watermelon for a necklace and bracelet in virtually no time. For earrings, just string beads on a head pin, make a wrapped loop, and attach an earring wire. Voilà — an entire stylish jewelry set of the moment, in a moment.

1 necklace • Cut a piece of beading wire (Basics, p. 12). On the wire, center a curved tube and enough seed beads to fill the tube.

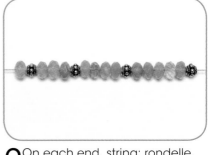

2 On each end, string: rondelle, 4–5 mm spacer, three rondelles, 4–5 mm spacer, four rondelles, 4–5 mm spacer, five rondelles, 4–5 mm spacer.

3 On each end, string six rondelles and a 4–5 mm spacer. String rondelles until the strand is within 1 in. (2.5 cm) of the finished length.

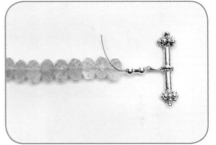

4 On each end, string a 3 mm spacer, a crimp bead, a 3 mm spacer, and half of a clasp. Check the fit, and add or remove beads if necessary. Go back through the beads just strung and tighten the wire. Crimp the crimp bead (Basics) and trim the excess wire.

1 bracelet • Cut a piece of beading wire (Basics, p. 12). Follow step 1 of the necklace.
On each end, string 4–5 mm spacers and rondelles until the strand is within 1 in. (2.5 cm) of the finished length.

2 On one end, string a 4–5 mm spacer, a crimp bead, a 3 mm spacer, and a lobster claw clasp. Repeat on the other end, substituting a 1¼-in. (3.2 cm) piece of chain for the clasp. Check the fit, and add or remove beads if necessary. Go back through the beads just strung and tighten the wire. Crimp the crimp beads (Basics) and trim the excess wire.

3 On a head pin, string a 3 mm spacer, a 4–5 mm spacer, and a rondelle. Make the first half of a wrapped loop (Basics). Attach the dangle and the end of the chain. Complete the wraps.

1 earrings • On a head pin, string: 4–5 mm spacer, rondelle, spacer, rondelle, spacer. If the spacers have large holes, string a 3 mm spacer first. Make a wrapped loop (Basics, p. 12).

2 Open the loop of an earring wire (Basics). Attach the dangle and close the loop. Make a second earring to match the first.

Design alternatives

To string a necklace with a less obvious focal point, center a silver bead and alternate with faceted rondelles (left). Or, group three silver beads in the center of your necklace (right) and alternate the types of spacers you use.

Tips

• Make sure to string seed beads to fill the curved tube. Otherwise, the tube won't align with the rondelles.

• If your 16-in. (41 cm) strand of rondelles does not have enough beads for a necklace, bracelet, and earrings, you can string more 4–5 mm spacers. If you're using sterling silver spacers, however, it may be more cost effective to buy two strands of gemstones up front.

Supplies

necklace 16½–17½ in. (41.9–44.5 cm)
- 50–60 mm curved silver tube bead
- 16-in. (41 cm) strand 8–9 mm faceted rondelles
- **15–20** 6º or 8º seed beads
- **10–12** 4–5 mm spacers
- **4** 3 mm round spacers
- flexible beading wire, .014 or .015
- **2** crimp beads
- toggle clasp
- chainnose or crimping pliers
- diagonal wire cutters

bracelet
- 50–60 mm curved silver tube bead
- **15–21** 8–9 mm faceted rondelles left over from necklace
- **15–20** 6º or 8º seed beads
- **7** 4–5 mm spacers
- **3** 3 mm round spacers
- flexible beading wire, .014 or .015
- 1½-in. (3.8 cm) head pin
- **2** crimp beads
- lobster claw clasp
- 1¼ in. (3.2 cm) chain for extender, 5–6 mm links
- chainnose and roundnose pliers
- diagonal wire cutters
- crimping pliers (optional)

earrings
- **4** 8–9 mm faceted rondelles
- **6** 4–5 mm spacers
- **2** 3 mm round spacers (optional)
- **2** 2-in. (5 cm) head pins
- pair of earring wires
- chainnose and roundnose pliers
- diagonal wire cutters

Frugal flight
of fancy

Make pretty, practical,
bird-themed jewelry

by Carol McKinney

Faceted
nuggets
for edgy style

Use chunky gemstones for a quick necklace and bracelet

by Naomi Fujimoto

This lepidolite jasper strand has a mix of purple, lavender, and beige that dazzles in its own right; I just added bicone crystals in "purple velvet" to play up the darker accents. After making a choker, I had one nugget left — perfect for a bracelet.

Supplies

necklace 15½ in. (39.4 cm)
- 16-in. (41 cm) strand 30–40 mm faceted nuggets
- **10–12** 5 or 6 mm bicone crystals
- **4** 3 mm round spacers
- flexible beading wire, .018 or .019
- 1½-in. (3.8 cm) head pin
- **2** crimp beads
- lobster claw clasp
- 3 in. (7.6 cm) chain for extender, 6–8 mm links

- chainnose and roundnose pliers
- diagonal wire cutters
- crimping pliers (optional)

bracelet
- 30–40 mm faceted nugget
- **4** 38 mm curved silver tube beads (Fire Mountain Gems and Beads, firemountaingems.com)
- **5–7** 5 or 6 mm bicone crystals
- **4** 3 mm round spacers

- flexible beading wire, .014 or .015
- 1½-in. (3.8 cm) head pin
- **2** crimp beads
- lobster claw clasp
- 1½-in. (3.8 cm) chain for extender, 6–8 mm links
- chainnose and roundnose pliers
- diagonal wire cutters
- crimping pliers (optional)

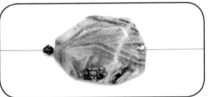

1 necklace • Cut a piece of beading wire (Basics, p. 12). String a bicone crystal and a faceted nugget. Repeat until the necklace is within 1 in. (2.5 cm) of the finished length, ending with a bicone.

2 On one end, string a spacer, a crimp bead, a spacer, and a lobster claw clasp. Repeat on the other end, substituting a 3-in. (7.6 cm) piece of chain for the clasp. Check the fit, and add or remove beads if necessary. Go back through the beads just strung and tighten the wire. Crimp the crimp beads (Basics) and trim the excess wire.

3 On a head pin, string a bicone. Make the first half of a wrapped loop (Basics). Attach the chain and complete the wraps.

1 bracelet • Cut two pieces of beading wire (Basics, p. 12). Over both wires, string a bicone crystal, a faceted nugget, and a bicone. Center the beads.

2 On each end of each wire, string a curved tube bead.

3 On one side, over both ends, string: one or two bicones, spacer, crimp bead, spacer, lobster claw clasp. Repeat on the other side, substituting a 1½-in. (3.8 cm) piece of chain for the clasp. Check the fit, and add or remove beads if necessary. Go back through the beads just strung and tighten the wires. Crimp the crimp beads (Basics) and trim the excess wire. Repeat step 3 of the necklace.

Tips
- "Lepidolite" is also commonly spelled "lapidalite."
- Because the nuggets are large, finish with a chain extender for flexibility in length.
- Another option: Try rich coffee jasper nuggets, crystal Dorado bicones, and gunmetal findings.

Earth
and sky
necklace

Turquoise accents brighten a neutral necklace and earrings

by Rupa Balachandar

Turquoise is a gorgeous stone, whether it's a focal point or an accent in a design. Here, I used it with silver beads to highlight an earthy palette for a necklace. I started my design with a carved-wood pendant and faceted Peruvian opals, then strung the turquoise toward the front of the necklace, where it will be most visible.

1 necklace • On a head pin, string a 3 mm spacer and a pendant. Make a wrapped loop (Basics, p. 12). Cut a piece of beading wire (Basics) and center the pendant.

2 On each end, string: metal accent bead, 4 mm spacer, oval bead, 4 mm spacer, bead cap, round bead, bead cap, 4 mm spacer, oval, 4 mm spacer.

3 On each end, string: bead cap, round, accent, round, bead cap, oval, 4 mm spacer, bead cap, round, bead cap, 4 mm spacer.

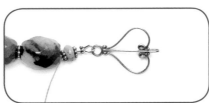

4 On each end, string an oval and a 4 mm spacer. Repeat until the necklace is within 1½ in. (3.8 cm) of the finished length. End with a 4 mm spacer.

5 On each end, string: rondelle, 4 mm spacer, crimp bead, 3 mm spacer, Wire Guardian, half of a clasp. Check the fit, and add or remove beads from each end if necessary. Go back through the beads just strung and tighten the wire. Crimp the crimp bead (Basics) and trim the excess wire.

❝These opals showcase a wonderful array of colors from white to brown with specks of caramel and black.❞

1 earrings • On a decorative head pin, string a bead cap, a round bead, a 4 mm spacer, and an oval bead. Make a wrapped loop (Basics, p. 12).

2 Open an earring wire (Basics). Attach the dangle and close the loop. Make a second earring to match the first.

Tip

Ask questions before you buy. That way, you can make sure that the strands you're considering aren't dyed howlite or magnesite. Also, avoid beads that look or feel like plastic, because they contain little turquoise and are mostly resin and dyes.

Design alternative

If you want turquoise to be more prominent in your design, string the necklace with faceted turquoise beads and use a brown gemstone (like bronzite) for the accents.

Supplies

necklace 20 in. (51 cm)
- 35–45 mm round pendant
- 16-in. (41 cm) strand 14–18 mm faceted oval beads
- **4** 8–12 mm metal accent beads
- **8** 10 mm round beads
- **2** 6–8 mm rondelles
- **26–30** 4 mm flat spacers
- **3** 3 mm flat spacers
- **12** 6–8 mm bead caps
- flexible beading wire, .014 or .015
- 3-in. (7.6 cm) head pin
- **2** crimp beads
- **2** Wire Guardians
- hook-and-eye clasp
- chainnose and roundnose pliers
- diagonal wire cutters
- crimping pliers (optional)

earrings
- **2** 14–18 mm faceted oval beads
- **2** 10 mm round beads
- **2** 4 mm flat spacers
- **2** 6–8 mm bead caps
- **2** 2½-in. (6.4 cm) decorative head pins
- pair of decorative earring wires
- chainnose and roundnose pliers
- diagonal wire cutters

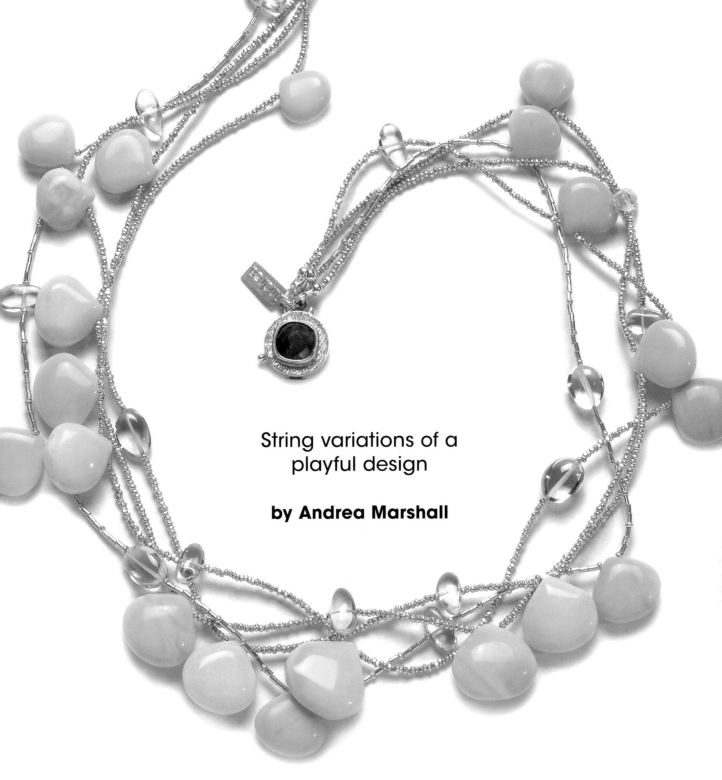

String variations of a
playful design

by Andrea Marshall

BLOOMING
inspiration

Steady drizzles of blue or silver seed beads, interspersed with beautiful briolette drops, call to mind the refreshing rainfall of a clear morning. Experiment with green seed beads and purple briolettes, and watch your creativity blossom into fashion.

1 necklace • Cut four pieces of beading wire (Basics, p. 12). On one wire, center a large briolette.

2 On each end of the first wire, string 3 in. (7.6 cm) of seed beads and a large briolette. Repeat until the strand is within 2 in. (5 cm) of the finished length.

3 On the second wire, center a large briolette. On each end, string 2 in. (5 cm) of seed beads, a small briolette, 2 in. (5 cm) of seed beads, and a large briolette. Repeat until the strand is within 2 in. (5 cm) of the finished length.

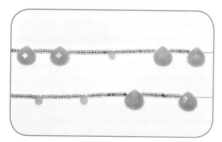

4 On the remaining two wires, string briolettes and seed beads as desired until each strand is within 2 in. (5 cm) of the finished length.

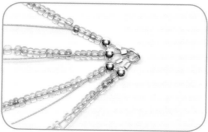

5 String a spacer and a crimp bead over each wire. Over all four wires, string a soldered jump ring. Repeat on the other side. Check the fit, and add or remove beads if necessary. Go back through the last few beads strung and tighten the wires. Crimp the crimp beads (Basics) and trim the excess wire.

6 On one side, open a jump ring (Basics) and attach the soldered jump ring and half of a clasp. Close the jump ring. Repeat on the other side.

Tips

• Use Wire Guardians, as in the silver seed bead necklace, if you are stringing heavy briolettes. The Wire Guardians will lend greater support to your piece.

• String seed beads not only in different colors, but in different cuts. I used bugle beads for one strand of the silver necklace.

• Make an asymmetrical necklace by spacing the briolettes at uneven intervals. Consider using accent beads in different shapes.

Design alternative

Use large briolettes left over from the necklace to create a second one. Choose colorful seed beads and smaller briolettes to complete the look.

1 earrings • Cut a 4-in. (10 cm) piece of wire. Center a large briolette. Bend the ends upward, crossing them into an X.

2 Make a set of wraps above the briolette (Basics, p. 12). Make a plain loop (Basics).

3 On a decorative head pin, string a small briolette. Curve the wire into an S shape, making a loop at the top.

4 Open the loop of an earring wire (Basics) and attach the dangles. Close the loop. Make a second earring to match the first.

Supplies

necklace 18 in. (46 cm)

◆ 16-in. (41 cm) strand 14–18 mm (large) briolettes
◆ 8-in. (20 cm) strand 4–5 mm (small) briolettes
◆ 15–20 g 8º seed beads
◆ **8** 4 mm spacers
◆ flexible beading wire, .014 or .015
◆ **2** 4–5 mm jump rings
◆ **2** 4–5 mm soldered jump rings
◆ **8** crimp beads
◆ box clasp
◆ chainnose and roundnose pliers, or **2** pairs of chainnose pliers
◆ diagonal wire cutters
◆ crimping pliers (optional)

earrings

◆ **2** 14–18 mm (large) briolettes
◆ **2** 4–5 mm (small) briolettes
◆ 8 in. (20 cm) 22-gauge half-hard wire
◆ **2** 2-in. (5 cm) decorative head pins
◆ pair of earring wires
◆ chainnose and roundnose pliers
◆ diagonal wire cutters

❝This necklace is one of a kind, but versatile. If you don't have the exact materials, you can still make something beautiful.❞

Bail out an unadorned drop pendant
with a leafy silver finding

by Roxie Moede

Turquoise suits

Starting with turquoise as the focal bead, I created two different designs. For summer, I added bright silver findings. In my fall version, jasper beads and oxidized chain play up the brown accents in the pendant. To get the most out of your 16-in. (41 cm) strand of beads, make a bracelet and earrings as well.

1 necklace • Use chainnose pliers to attach a bail to a top-drilled drop or briolette. Cut a 3–4-in. (7.6–10 cm) piece of chain. Center the pendant on the chain.

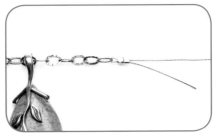

2 Cut two 9–11-in. (23–28 cm) pieces of beading wire. On each wire, string a crimp bead, a spacer, and one end of the chain. Go back through the beads just strung and tighten the wire. Crimp the crimp bead (Basics, p. 12) and trim the excess wire.

3 On each end, string two round beads and a spacer. Repeat until the necklace is within 1 in. (2.5 cm) of the finished length.

4 On one end, string a spacer, a crimp bead, a spacer, and a lobster claw clasp. Repeat on the other end, substituting a 3-in. (7.6 cm) piece of chain for the clasp. Check the fit, and add or remove beads if necessary. Go back through the last few beads strung and tighten the wire. Crimp the crimp beads and trim the excess wire.

Supplies

necklace 15½ in. (39.4 cm)
- 30 mm top-drilled drop or briolette
- 16-in. (41 cm) strand 8 mm round beads
- **20–26** 2–3 mm spacers
- pinch bail with side prongs
- flexible beading wire, .014 or .015
- 7–8 in. (18–20 cm) chain, 4–6 mm links
- **4** crimp beads
- lobster claw clasp
- chainnose and crimping pliers
- diagonal wire cutters

bracelet
- **8–11** 8 mm round beads
- 6–8 in. (15–20 cm) chain, 4–6 mm links
- **8–11** 1½-in. (3.8 cm) head pins
- **10–13** 3–4 mm jump rings
- lobster claw clasp and soldered jump ring
- chainnose and roundnose pliers
- diagonal wire cutters

earrings
- **4** 8 mm round beads
- 3 in. (7.6 cm) chain, 4–6 mm links
- **4** 1½-in. (3.8 cm) head pins
- **2** 3–4 mm jump rings
- pair of lever-back earring wires
- chainnose and roundnose pliers
- diagonal wire cutters

any season

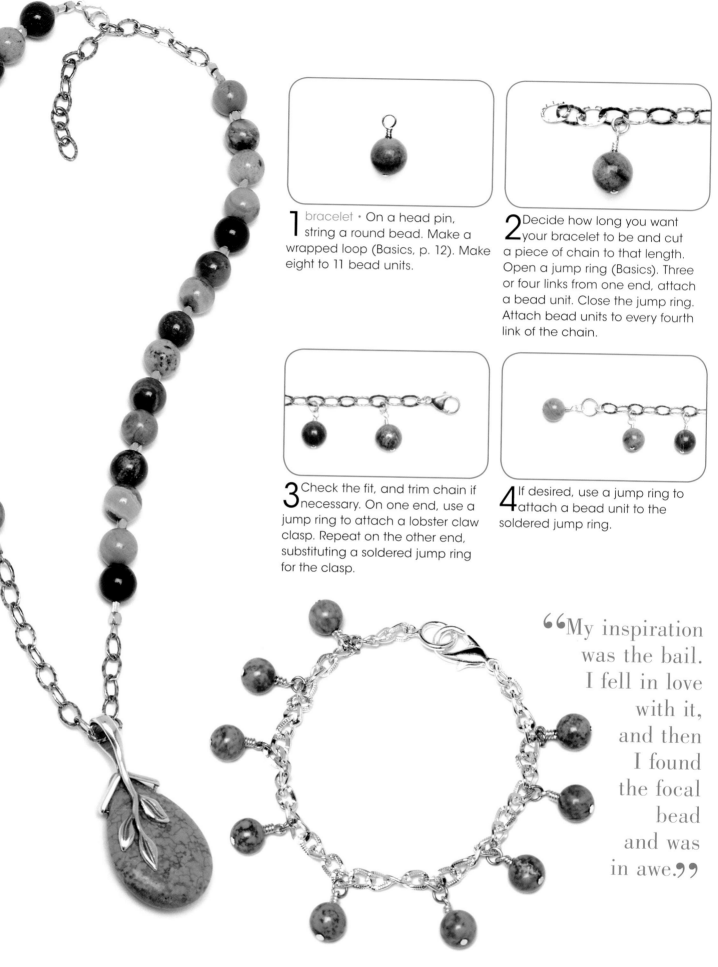

1 bracelet • On a head pin, string a round bead. Make a wrapped loop (Basics, p. 12). Make eight to 11 bead units.

2 Decide how long you want your bracelet to be and cut a piece of chain to that length. Open a jump ring (Basics). Three or four links from one end, attach a bead unit. Close the jump ring. Attach bead units to every fourth link of the chain.

3 Check the fit, and trim chain if necessary. On one end, use a jump ring to attach a lobster claw clasp. Repeat on the other end, substituting a soldered jump ring for the clasp.

4 If desired, use a jump ring to attach a bead unit to the soldered jump ring.

"My inspiration was the bail. I fell in love with it, and then I found the focal bead and was in awe."

1 earrings • On a head pin, string a round bead. Make a plain loop (Basics, p. 12). Make a second bead unit.

2 Cut a ½-in. (1.3 cm) and a 1-in. (2.5 cm) piece of chain. Open the loop of each bead unit (Basics) and attach the end link of a chain. Close the loops.

3 Open a jump ring (Basics). Attach both chains and the loop of an earring wire. Close the jump ring. Make a second earring to match the first.

Design alternative

This design lends itself to virtually any combination of materials. I also made a version with a faceted agate pendant and shimmery multicolored pearls.

Tip

Try to find a drop that has less than 10 mm between the holes and the top of the pendant. If you have trouble attaching the bail, let the bail fall in front of the pendant, and use chainnose pliers to bend the loop back slightly.

Everyday

Earth-toned jewels are perfect for a fall wardrobe

by Eva Kapitany

Agate and jasper beads, with their brilliant bands and spots of color, come in a variety of stunning cuts. These earthy jewels lean toward the elegant when paired with gold chain. Mix stones of different sizes and shapes for a necklace soon to be your wardrobe's principal player.

elegance

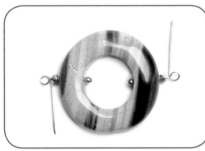

1 On a head pin, string a round spacer, an inside hole of a donut, and a faceted spacer. Make the first half of a wrapped loop (Basics, p. 12). Repeat with the donut's remaining hole. Make four donut units.

2 Cut a 4½-in. (11.4 cm) piece of wire. Make the first half of a wrapped loop on one end. String: round spacer, bead cap or flat spacer, gemstone bead, bead cap or flat spacer, round spacer. Make the first half of a wrapped loop. Make six to 10 bead units.

3 Cut 10 to 14 1-in. (2.5 cm) pieces of chain. Attach a loop of a donut unit and a chain and complete the wraps. Attach the remaining bead units, chains, and donut units, completing the wraps as you go. Attach the last chain to the first donut unit.

Tip

In step 2, it's not necessary to cut a 4½-in. (11.4 cm) piece of wire for every bead. For beads smaller than 35 mm, 3-in. (7.6 cm) pieces of wire should be adequate.

Design alternative

Base metal chain and five beads placed just at the front of this necklace make it a less expensive (and quicker) option.

Supplies

necklace (34–38 in./86–97 cm)

- ◆ **6-10** 20–70 mm gemstone beads
- ◆ **4** 30–50 mm gemstone donuts, with two holes
- ◆ **6-12** 6 mm flat spacers
- ◆ **8** 4 mm faceted spacers
- ◆ **20-28** 3 mm round spacers
- ◆ **12-20** 6–12 mm bead caps
- ◆ 27–45 in. (69–1.1 m) 24-gauge half-hard wire
- ◆ 10–14 in. (25–36 cm) chain, 3–4 mm links
- ◆ **8** 3-in. (7.6 cm) head pins
- ◆ chainnose and roundnose pliers
- ◆ diagonal wire cutters

Tip

Beads between 30–60 mm balance an extra-long necklace.

66I often find myself designing jewelry into the early morning hours.99

Down-
to-earth

A geode pendant is a natural adornment

by Carol McKinney

The word "geode" comes from the Greek word *geoides*, which means earth-like. A geode is a geological rock formation, and those completely filled with compact crystal formations are called nodules. The exquisite color, banding, and natural shape of the top-drilled agate slices make them extraordinary pendants.

1 necklace • Cut a piece of beading wire (Basics, p. 12). On one end, string a spacer, a crimp bead, a Wire Guardian, and half of a clasp. Go back through the beads just strung and tighten the wire.

2 String 2 in. (5 cm) of 6–10 mm beads.

3 Attach a pinch bail to a geode and string it on the wire.

"It's just amazing to me how beautiful God has made nature for us to enjoy, and even wear."

4 String beads until the strand is within 1 in. (2.5 cm) of the finished length. String a spacer, a crimp bead, a Wire Guardian, and the other half of the clasp. Check the fit, and add or remove beads if necessary. Go back through the last few beads strung and tighten the wire. Make folded crimps (Basics) and trim the excess wire.

5 Using the outer notch of your crimping pliers, gently close a crimp cover over each crimp.

Tip

If your pendant is more than 5 mm thick, you will need to substitute a large jump ring or wire for the pinch bail.

necklace

Supplies

**necklace (brown geode
17 in./43 cm; green geode
18½ in./47 cm)**
- 60–70 mm geode pendant
- **55–65** 6–10 mm beads
- **2** 3 mm round spacers
- pinch bail
- flexible beading wire, .014 or .015
- **2** crimp beads
- **2** crimp covers
- **2** Wire Guardians
- clasp (mermaid clasp by Carl
  Clasmeyer, clasmeyer.com)
- crimping pliers
- diagonal wire cutters

bracelet
- 37 mm marquise-shaped link
- **34–44** 6–10 mm beads
- **4** 3 mm round spacers
- flexible beading wire, .014 or .015
- **4** crimp beads
- **4** crimp covers
- **4** Wire Guardians
- lobster claw clasp
- crimping pliers
- diagonal wire cutters
- bench block or anvil
- hammer

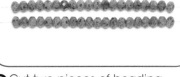

1 bracelet • On a bench block or anvil, hammer a marquise-shaped link. Turn the link over and hammer the other side.

2 Cut two pieces of beading wire (Basics, p. 12). String 6–10 mm beads until the strands are within 2½ in. (6.4 cm) of the finished length.

3 On one side, over each wire, string a spacer, a crimp bead, and a Wire Guardian. Over both wires, string a lobster claw clasp. Go back through the last few beads strung and tighten the wires. Make folded crimps (Basics) and trim the excess wire.

4 Check the fit, and add or remove beads if necessary. Repeat step 3 on the other side, substituting the link for the clasp. Repeat step 5 of the necklace.

Design alternative

You can save a few dollars by omitting the fancy clasp. String two strands of 3–4 mm beads on one side of the pendant and one strand of 6–8 mm beads on the other. Finish with a lobster claw clasp.

Customize
a necklace for
a special
friend

by Lindsay Hastings

Off-center accent

A square gemstone lends a surprising pop of color. Whether you start with a strand of gemstone chips or opt for more substantial nuggets, a single contrasting bead perfects this offbeat design. Make coiled bicone units in the same shade as your gemstones, or mix several bicone colors for added sparkle. A sister who gardens will appreciate a silver flower pendant, or for a beachcombing buddy, choose a massive Hill Tribe shell to anchor this unconventional necklace.

Supplies

necklace (gold shell pendant 16 in./41 cm; silver flower pendant 21 in./53 cm)

- ◆ 60 mm Hill Tribe pendant
- ◆ 20–26 mm accent bead
- ◆ 16-in. (41 cm) strand 8–12 mm gemstone chips
- ◆ **18–21** 4 mm bicone crystals
- ◆ **2** 4 mm spacers (optional)
- ◆ flexible beading wire, .018 or .019
- ◆ 36 in. (91 cm) 24-gauge half-hard wire
- ◆ 6 in. (15 cm) 20-gauge half-hard wire (optional)
- ◆ **4** 4 mm jump rings
- ◆ **2** crimp beads
- ◆ **2** Wire Guardians
- ◆ toggle or hook-and-eye clasp
- ◆ chainnose and roundnose pliers
- ◆ diagonal wire cutters
- ◆ crimping pliers (optional)

1 Cut a 2-in. (5 cm) piece of 24-gauge wire. Make a coil on one end. String a bicone and make a wrapped loop (Basics, p. 12). Make 16–20 bicone units.

2 Open a jump ring (Basics) and attach four or five bicone units. Close the jump ring. Make four jump ring units.

3 For a drilled pendant without a bail, cut a 6-in. (15 cm) piece of 20-gauge wire. Make a coil on one end. String a pendant and a bicone. Make a wrapped loop.
Cut a piece of beading wire (Basics). Center the pendant.

4 On one end, string 1 in. (2.5 cm) of chips, two jump ring units, an accent bead, and two jump ring units.

5 On each end, string chips until the strand is within 1 in. (2.5 cm) of the finished length.

6 On each end, string a spacer or bicone, a crimp bead, a Wire Guardian, and half of a clasp. Check the fit, and add or remove beads if necessary. Go back through the last few beads strung and tighten the wire. Crimp the crimp bead (Basics) and trim the excess wire.

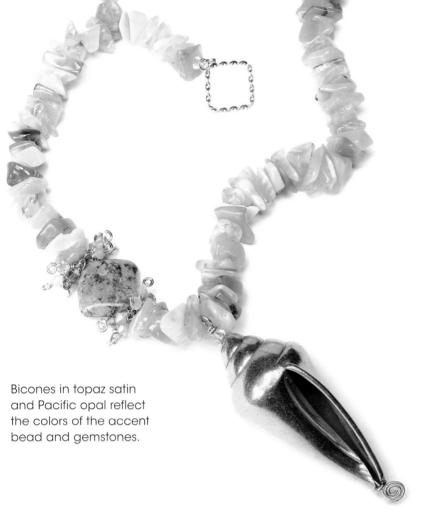

Bicones in topaz satin and Pacific opal reflect the colors of the accent bead and gemstones.

Tip

Before you begin, cut 16 to 20 2-in. (5 cm) pieces of wire and make a coil on one end of each. Then string the bicones and make plain loops on each.

"Too much emphasis is put on symmetry."

Design alternative

For this quick purple version, choose an accent bead to match the color of the chips. The ornate silver end caps add just enough detail, so the bicone units are not necessary.

A collection of
different shapes
comes together
in a necklace

by Monica Lueder

Creative
curves

Combine an assortment of shapes and textures with a unifying
roundness: Try circular links, puffed squares, and onion-shaped
briolettes for a soft yet geometric necklace.

1 Cut a 1¼-in. (3.2 cm) piece of wire. Make a plain loop (Basics, p. 12) on one end. String a square bead and make a plain loop. Repeat, substituting a bead cap, saucer, and bead cap for the square. Make 24 to 30 square units and eight to 10 saucer units.

2 Cut a 1½-in. (3.8 cm) piece of wire. Make a plain loop. String two briolettes. Turn them in opposite directions and make a plain loop perpendicular to the first loop. Make four or five briolette units.

3 Open a jump ring (Basics). Attach two round links and close the jump ring. Use a jump ring to attach a third round link. Make eight to 10 round-link segments.

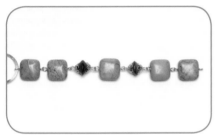

4 Open one loop (Basics) of a square unit. Attach one end of a round-link segment and close the loop. Attach: second loop of the square unit, square unit, saucer unit, square unit, saucer unit, two square units.

5 On the square unit's loop, attach a round-link segment, a square unit, and a briolette unit.

6 Repeat the patterns in steps 4 and 5, attaching round-link segments and bead units until the necklace is the desired length, ending with a square unit. Attach the loop of the last square unit to the first round-link segment.

Design alternative

Try pre-connected links for oversized earrings. Brushed vermeil links from The Earth Bazaar, theearthbazaar.com.

Supplies

necklace 45 in. (1.1 m)
- **24–30** 13–15 mm square beads
- **8–10** 12–15 mm briolettes
- **8–10** 8–12 mm saucers
- **16–20** 7 mm bead caps
- **24–30** 20 mm round links
- **4–5 ft. (1.2–1.5 m)** 24-gauge half-hard wire
- **16–20** 6–7 mm jump rings
- chainnose and roundnose pliers
- diagonal wire cutters

"I'm a dabbler, so I think that's why I enjoy doing so many different things. I never seem to stick to one specific style."

Moss agate
and aragonite
beads make
the carnelian
pendant pop.

Earth-toned ensemble

A carnelian pendant invites a warm palette

by Sara Strauss

The starting point for my design was the color and shape of the pendant. (I'd suggest choosing the pendant first.) I liked how the moss agate briolettes match the shape of the pendant and the creamy aragonite beads soften the overall look. I used a few leftover beads, including red aventurine, to make matching earrings.

Supplies

necklace 15½ in. (39.4 cm)
- 40–50 mm drop or briolette pendant
- 16-in. (41 cm) strand 11–13 mm briolettes
- **24–32** 6 mm faceted round beads, **2** color A, **12–16** color B, **10–12** color C
- **12–16** 4 mm bicone crystals
- flexible beading wire, .014 or .015
- 3 in. (7.6 cm) 24-gauge half-hard wire
- **2** crimp beads
- toggle clasp
- chainnose and roundnose pliers
- diagonal wire cutters
- crimping pliers (optional)

earrings
- **2** 11–13 mm briolettes
- **2** 6 mm faceted round beads
- **2** 4 mm round beads
- 10 in. (25 cm) 24-gauge half-hard wire
- pair of earring wires
- chainnose and roundnose pliers
- diagonal wire cutters

1 necklace • Cut a 3-in. (7.6 cm) piece of 24-gauge wire. String a pendant and make a set of wraps above it (Basics, p. 12). Make a wrapped loop (Basics) perpendicular to the pendant.

2 Cut a piece of beading wire (Basics). Center the pendant. On each end, string a color A round bead, a bicone crystal, and a color B round bead.

❝I prefer silver to gold, and in general I love bright colors, which are more fun to work with.❞

3 On each end, string two 11–13 mm briolettes, a color C round bead, a bicone, and a color B. Repeat until the strand is within 1 in. (2.5 cm) of the finished length.

4 On each end, string a crimp bead and half of a clasp. Check the fit, and add or remove beads if necessary. Go back through the last few beads strung and tighten the wire. Crimp the crimp bead (Basics) and trim the excess wire.

1 earrings • Cut a 3-in. (7.6 cm) piece of 24-gauge wire. String an 11–13 mm briolette and make a set of wraps above it (Basics, p. 12). Make a wrapped loop (Basics) perpendicular to the briolette.

2 Cut a 1-in. (2.5 cm) piece of wire. Make a plain loop (Basics) on one end. String a 4 mm bead and make a plain loop perpendicular to the first loop. Make a second bead unit, substituting a 6 mm bead, with the plain loops parallel to each other.

3 Open each loop (Basics) of the 6 mm-bead unit. Attach the loop of the briolette unit and one loop of the 4 mm-bead unit. Close the loops.

4 Open the loop of an earring wire and attach the dangle. Close the loop. Make a second earring to match the first.

Tiger eye for style

Make an attention-getting necklace with bold square gemstones

by Erin Dolan

I've always thought that navy was an underrated neutral, lost in black or brown's shadow. So I was delighted to find these stones in a rich, deep blue. When they are strung in an asymmetrical pattern with simple seed beads, all eyes are on the tiger eye.

1 necklace • Cut a piece of beading wire (Basics, p. 12) for the shortest strand of your necklace. Cut two more pieces, each 2 in. (5 cm) longer than the previous piece. On the longest wire, center a tiger eye bead.

2 On each end, string seed beads interspersed with Czech glass beads, 5 mm silver beads, and 4 mm silver beads until the strand is within 2 in. (5 cm) of the finished length.

3 On the middle wire, string a tiger eye bead. On one end, string 4 in. (10 cm) of beads as in step 2. On the other end, string 10 in. (25 cm) of beads.

On the shortest wire, string a tiger eye bead, eight seed beads, and a tiger eye bead. On one end, string 3 in. (7.6 cm) of beads. On the other end, string 8 in. (20 cm) of beads.

4 Cut a 4-in. (10 cm) piece of 22-gauge wire. On one end, make a wrapped loop (Basics). Repeat.

On each end, over each wire, string a crimp bead, two seed beads, and the loop. Check the fit, and add or remove beads if necessary. Go back through the last few beads strung and tighten the wire. Crimp the crimp bead (Basics) and trim the excess wire.

5 On each end, string a cone and two seed beads. Make the first half of a wrapped loop. Attach half of a clasp and complete the wraps.

Tip

The 4 mm faceted silver beads shown here are Karen Hill Tribe Silver spacers. Use an assortment of beads, shapes, and colors in your own version. This design is great for using up materials left over from other projects.

1 bracelet • **a** Cut two pieces of beading wire (Basics, p. 12).

b On one end, over each wire, string a crimp bead, two seed beads, and half of a clasp. Go back through the beads just strung and tighten the wire. Crimp the crimp bead (Basics) and trim the excess wire.

2 On each wire, string 3 in. (7.6 cm) of seed beads, Czech glass beads, and silver beads. Over both wires, string a tiger eye bead.

3 String beads as desired until the strands are within 2 in. (5 cm) of the finished length. On each end, over each wire, string a crimp bead, two seed beads, and half of a clasp. Check the fit, and add or remove beads if necessary. Go back through the last few beads strung and tighten the wire. Crimp the crimp bead (Basics) and trim the excess wire.

1 earrings • On a head pin, string a Czech glass bead, an 8º seed bead, a silver bead, and two 11º seed beads. Make a plain loop (Basics, p. 12).

2 Open the loop of an earring wire (Basics) and attach the dangle. Make a second earring to match the first.

Design alternative

For a sleeker look on a slimmer budget, string one tiger eye bead instead of four. A monochromatic color palette makes the square shape the star of the necklace.

Supplies

necklace 18 in. (46 cm)
- **4** 20–30 mm square tiger eye beads
- **1** or **2** 11-in. (28 cm) strands 5 mm Czech glass beads
- **10–20** 5 mm round silver beads
- **10–20** 4 mm faceted silver beads (Artbeads.com)
- 5–10 g 8º seed beads
- 5–10 g 8º hex-cut seed beads
- 5–10 g 11º seed beads
- flexible beading wire, .014 or .015
- 8 in. (20 cm) 22-gauge half-hard wire
- **2** cones
- **6** crimp beads
- toggle clasp
- chainnose and roundnose pliers
- diagonal wire cutters
- crimping pliers (optional)

bracelet
- 20–30 mm square tiger eye bead
- **10** 5 mm Czech glass beads
- **5** 5 mm round silver beads
- **5** 4 mm faceted silver beads
- 1 g 8º seed beads
- 1 g 8º hex-cut seed beads
- 1 g 11º seed beads
- flexible beading wire, .014 or .015
- **4** crimp beads
- toggle clasp
- chainnose and roundnose pliers
- diagonal wire cutters
- crimping pliers (optional)

earrings
- **2** 5 mm Czech glass beads
- **2** 4 mm faceted silver beads
- **2** 8º seed beads
- **4** 11º seed beads
- **2** 2-in. (5 cm) head pins
- pair of earring wires
- chainnose and roundnose pliers
- diagonal wire cutters

❝ I created this necklace as I would create an outfit. It's all about balance.**❞**

1

necklace
Use heavy-duty wire cutters to cut a piece of chain to the finished length.

BIG BOLD BRIOLETTES

Let loose with eye-catching beads

by Naomi Fujimoto

Wrapped loops are wonderful — their lollipop roundness, their wraps symmetrically aligned on the stem. But when playing around with oversized briolettes, challenge yourself to design something less traditional — and more consistent with chunky industrial-looking chain. So, for the design on page 58, wrap the briolettes casually. The look is stylish — and as a bonus, these wraps take less time than more formal wraps. The necklace on page 57 is even easier to make: Simply string the big briolettes and attach them to a chain.

5 On one end, use a jump ring (Basics) to attach a lobster claw clasp. On the other end, attach a round-bead unit.

4 On each end, string a spacer, a crimp, and a spacer. Attach each end to a chain link and crimp the crimp beads (Basics, p. 12).

3 On each end, alternate a spacer with a briolette, until you've strung all the briolettes.

2 Cut a 13-in. (33 cm) piece of beading wire. Center the largest briolette.

Supplies

blue necklace 19 in. (48 cm)
- **11–13** 25–40 mm briolettes
- 10 mm round bead
- **14–16** 3–4 mm spacers
- flexible beading wire, .018 or .019
- 17–21 in. (43–53 cm) chain, 10–14 mm links
- 2-in. (5 cm) decorative head pin
- 7–10 mm 16- or 18-gauge jump ring
- **2** crimp beads
- 20–24 mm lobster claw clasp
- chainnose and roundnose pliers
- diagonal wire cutters
- heavy-duty wire cutters
- crimping pliers (optional)

clear earrings
- **2** 25–30 mm briolettes
- 40 in. (1 m) 24-gauge half-hard wire
- pair of earring wires
- chainnose and roundnose pliers
- diagonal wire cutters

clear necklace 17 in. (43 cm)
- **5** 25–30 mm briolettes
- 12 in. (30 cm) 20-gauge half-hard wire
- 80 in. (2 m) 22-gauge half-hard wire
- 15–19 in. (38–48 cm) chain, 15–18 mm links
- 24 mm lobster claw clasp
- chainnose and roundnose pliers
- diagonal wire cutters
- heavy-duty wire cutters

clear bracelet
- 25–30 mm briolette
- 24 in. (61 cm) 20-gauge half-hard wire
- 16 in. (41 cm) 22-gauge half-hard wire
- 6–8 in. (15–20 cm) chain, 15–18 mm links
- 20–24 mm lobster claw clasp
- chainnose and roundnose pliers
- diagonal wire cutters
- heavy-duty wire cutters

Tips

• The thinner the wire, the longer the piece you'll need to create prominent wraps.
• If you don't have heavy-duty wire cutters, you can use two pairs of chainnose pliers to open and remove links of chain. If you opt to use pliers, use household pliers (rather than your jewelry pliers).

"By clustering big briolettes or making free-form wire wraps, you can give your necklace an architectural feel."

Design alternative

If you have inexpensive briolettes that don't have a consistent shape, string them in a bracelet.

ROCKER
chic

Pair mismatched agate slices for earrings that rock

by Sara Strauss

I love designing with agate. Its bands of color inspire me to meld pinks, purples, browns, and greys. Though these Botswana agate earrings do not match, each slice is distinctly beautiful. Accentuate the subdued shades of these mismatched slices by dangling them from a few matching beads.

1 Cut a 3-in. (7.6 cm) piece of 24-gauge wire. String an agate slice and make a set of wraps above it (Basics, p. 12). Make a wrapped loop (Basics).

2 Cut a 1¼-in. (3.2 cm) piece of 22-gauge wire. Make a plain loop (Basics) on one end. String a rondelle and make a plain loop. Repeat with a round bead.

3 Open the loops (Basics) of the rondelle unit. Attach one loop to the loop of the slice. Attach the other loop to a loop of the round-bead unit. Close the loops.

4 Open the loop of an earring wire and attach the dangle. Close the loop. Make a second earring to match the first.

Supplies

- **2** 55 mm agate slices
- **2** 10 mm rondelles
- **2** 8 mm round beads
- 5 in. (13 cm) 22-gauge half-hard wire
- 6 in. (15 cm) 24-gauge half-hard wire
- pair of earring wires
- chainnose and roundnose pliers
- diagonal wire cutters

Crystals

Cascading color

A striking monochromatic flow of beads creates drama

by Monica Lueder

Whether you choose waves of molten red or bracing icy blue, this necklace-and-earrings set is an eye-catcher. Adjust the length of the dangles or even the number of strands to fit a particular neckline or mood.

1 necklace • On a head pin, string a rondelle. Make a plain loop (Basics, p. 12). Make 29 rondelle units.

2 Cut a 1-in. (2.5 cm) piece of wire. Make a plain loop. String a 6 mm crystal and make a plain loop. Make 42 6 mm units.

3 Cut a 1-in. (2.5 cm) piece of wire. Make a plain loop. String a 4 mm bead or crystal and make a plain loop. Make 29 4 mm units.

4 Open the loops (Basics) of a 6 mm unit. Attach a rondelle unit to one loop and a 4 mm unit to the other. Close the loops. Make 16 short dangles. Make 13 long dangles by attaching an additional 6 mm unit as shown.

5 To make the top strand: Cut a 15-in. (38 cm) piece of chain. Center two short dangles on the chain, leaving three links open between them.

On each side, attach five short dangles, leaving three links open between each.

6 Cut an 18-in. (46 cm) piece of chain. Attach a long dangle to the center link.

7 On each side, attach six long dangles and two short dangles, leaving three links open between each dangle.

8 Open a jump ring (Basics). Attach one end of each chain and a lobster claw clasp. Close the jump ring. Repeat on the other end, substituting a soldered jump ring for the clasp.

1 earrings • Following necklace steps 1 to 4, make a short dangle. Cut a 1¾-in. (4.4 cm) and a ¾-in. (1.9 cm) piece of chain.

2 Open the loop of an earring wire (Basics, p. 12). Attach the dangle and the chains. Close the loop. Make a second earring in the mirror image of the first.

Supplies

necklace 18 in. (46 cm)
- **29** 9 mm cathedral fire-polished rondelles
- **42** 6 mm round crystals
- **29** 4 mm round beads or crystals
- **71** in. (1.8 m) 22-gauge half-hard wire
- **33** in. (84 cm) chain, 2–3 mm links
- **29** 1½-in. (3.8 cm) head pins
- **2** 7 mm jump rings
- lobster claw clasp and soldered jump ring
- chainnose and roundnose pliers
- diagonal wire cutters

earrings
- **2** 9 mm cathedral fire-polished rondelles
- **2** 6 mm round crystals
- **2** 4 mm round beads or crystals
- **4** in. (10 cm) 22-gauge half-hard wire
- **6** in. (15 cm) chain, 2–3 mm links
- **2** 1½-in. (3.8 cm) head pins
- pair of earring wires
- chainnose and roundnose pliers
- diagonal wire cutters

Design alternative

Use a beaded strand instead of chain and shorten the dangles. The look is compact and lush.

Editor's Tips

• For the red necklace, use 4 mm bicone crystals and 6 mm crystals in two colors. The topaz crystals mimic the cathedral finish of the rondelles. For the blue version, keep a calming monochromatic palette.
• To save time, use eye pins instead of wire for the dangles.
• Your dangles may vary in length because of slight differences in loop size. Before attaching the dangles to the chain, line up both sets and make sure the longer ones are in the center.

Autumn leaves

Crystals and WireLace play with fall light

by Linda Arline Hartung

The vision of delicate autumn leaves stirred by this gorgeous bracelet-and-earrings set is welcome any time of the year. While most sets revolve around a necklace, these earrings and bracelet will be sure to draw attention.

1 bracelet • On a crystal-studded head pin, string a leaf-shaped crystal. Bend the head pin back over the top of the leaf at a 45-degree angle.

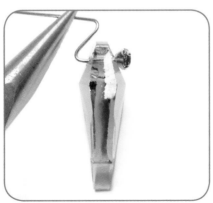

2 About ¼ in. (6 mm) from the first bend, bend the wire away from the leaf at a 45-degree angle.

3 Use roundnose pliers to grip the head pin at the second bend. Wrap the wire around the jaws of your roundnose pliers to make half of a loop. Make three half-wrapped leaf units.

4 On a head pin, string a 4 mm bicone crystal, a 6 mm bicone crystal, and an 8 mm bicone crystal. Make the first half of a wrapped loop (Basics, p. 12). Make 12 bicone units, completing the wraps on two of the units.

5 Cut a piece of chain with 11 crystal units, leaving a link on each end. Attach a leaf unit to every third link. Wrap the head pins as shown and trim the excess wire.

Supplies

bracelet 7¾ in. (19.7 cm)
- ◆ **3** 26 mm leaf-shaped crystals
- ◆ **12** 8 mm bicone crystals, top-drilled
- ◆ **12** 6 mm bicone crystals, top-drilled
- ◆ **12** 4 mm bicone crystals
- ◆ **1** yd. (.9 m) 6 mm WireLace
- ◆ **7** in. (18 cm) crystal chain
- ◆ **3** 1½-in. (3.8 cm) crystal-studded head pins
- ◆ **12** 2-in. (5 cm) head pins
- ◆ leaf clasp
- ◆ chainnose pliers
- ◆ roundnose pliers
- ◆ diagonal wire cutters
- ◆ two-part epoxy

earrings
- ◆ **2** 26 mm leaf-shaped crystals
- ◆ **2** 8 mm bicone crystals, top-drilled
- ◆ **4** 6 mm bicone crystals, top-drilled
- ◆ **2** 4 mm bicone crystals
- ◆ **2** 1½-in. (3.8 cm) crystal-studded head pins
- ◆ **2** 2-in. (5 cm) head pins
- ◆ **2** 4 mm jump rings
- ◆ pair of cup-and-post earrings with ear nuts
- ◆ chainnose pliers
- ◆ roundnose pliers
- ◆ diagonal wire cutters
- ◆ two-part epoxy

Kits available from Alacarte Clasps, alacarteclasps.com.

6 Attach a half-wrapped bicone unit to each link between the crystal links. Complete the wraps. On each end, open the link and attach a wrapped bicone unit and half of a clasp. Close the link.

7 Cut a 10-in. (25 cm) piece of WireLace. String an end link of the chain and tie two overhand knots (Basics) around the link.

8 Weave the lace through each link, tying overhand knots next to each bicone unit as you go. Insert your finger between the chain and the lace as you tie knots, creating loops. Apply two-part epoxy to the end knots and trim the excess lace.

9 Gently pull apart the WireLace loops to create waves.

Tip

When making the crystal leaf units, place your roundnose pliers against the crystal leaf before bending the head pin back to avoid cracking the hole around the crystal.

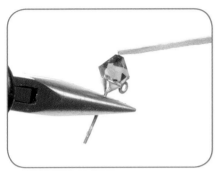

1 earrings • Apply two-part epoxy to the cup of an earring post. Insert the hole end of a 6 mm top-drilled bicone in the cup.

2 Following bracelet steps 1 to 3, make a leaf unit. Complete the wraps.

Design alternative

Replace the leaf-shaped crystals with filigree foliage to match the delicacy of the WireLace.

3 On a head pin, string a 4 mm bicone crystal, a 6 mm bicone crystal, and an 8 mm bicone crystal. Make a wrapped loop (Basics, p. 12).

4 Open a jump ring (Basics). Attach the leaf unit, the bicone unit, and the loop of the earring post. Close the jump ring. Make a second earring to match the first.

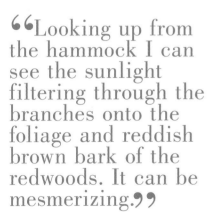

"Looking up from the hammock I can see the sunlight filtering through the branches onto the foliage and reddish brown bark of the redwoods. It can be mesmerizing."

Tip

Despite the number of steps, the techniques used in this project are relatively simple. If you plan to make both pieces, keep things organized by making the leaf and bicone dangles all at once.

Cheeky chic

A faux diamond ring winks at its expensive cousins

by Monica Han

There's no powder blue box in sight, but an inexpensive cubic zirconia earring and some wire wrapping will still give you that store-bought feeling. This witty interpretation of a solitaire ring turns ordinary wirework into something special.

1 Trim the post from a cubic zirconia (CZ) earring as close to the setting as possible.

2 Cut a 34-in. (86 cm) piece of wire. Wrap the wire four times around a mandrel or your finger at the desired ring size. String the wire through the CZ setting and wrap the wire around the mandrel once more.

Supplies

- cubic zirconia post earring
- 34 in. (86 cm) 22-gauge half-hard wire
- diagonal wire cutters
- ring mandrel (optional)

Tip

Get a feel for wire wrapping by practicing with inexpensive, malleable copper wire.

3 Remove the mandrel. On one side of the CZ setting, wrap the wire around the ring-base loops four times.

4 Wrap the wire around the base of the CZ setting until there is about 4 in. (10 cm) remaining.

Design alternative

String several small components on your ring when you're not in a "big rock" mood.

5 On the other side of the CZ setting, wrap the wire around the ring-base loops and trim the excess wire.

"My favorite wireworking tips are practice, practice, practice, and be consistent."

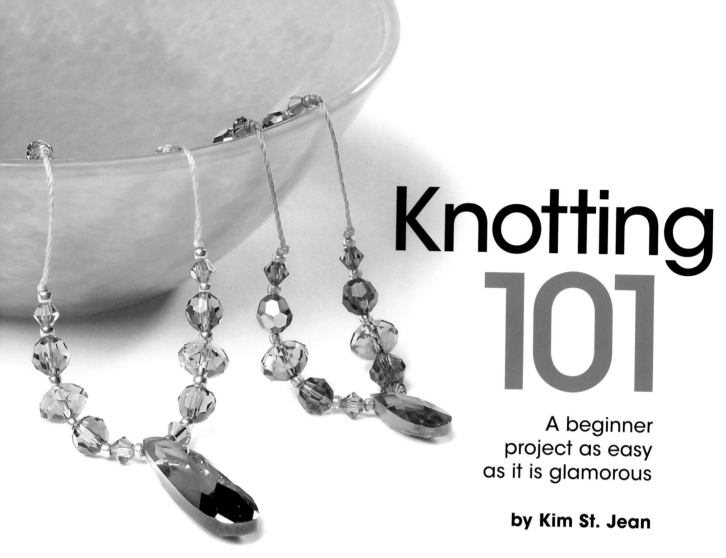

Knotting 101

A beginner project as easy as it is glamorous

by Kim St. Jean

If you want a novice knotting project, this is the one for you. It looks great and is simple to build around the sleek shape of a CZ drop. This elegant necklace and earrings set will garner so much attention, you might want to make sets in lots of different color combinations.

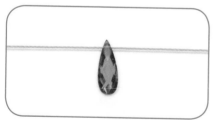

1 necklace • Cut an 18–24-in. (46–61 cm) piece of thread or braiding string. Center a pendant.

2 On each end, string: 11º seed bead, bicone crystal, 11º, round crystal, 11º, crystal rondelle, 11º, round, 11º, bicone, 11º. Tie an overhand knot (Basics, p. 12) next to the last 11º.

3a On each side, about 1 in. (2.5 cm) from the knot, tie an overhand knot.

b Repeat steps 2 and 3a until the necklace is within 1 in. (2.5 cm) of the finished length.

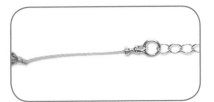

4 Check the fit and trim the excess thread. Apply glue and string a crimp end. Flatten the crimp portion of the crimp end (Basics).

Open a jump ring (Basics). Attach a lobster claw clasp and the crimp end. Close the jump ring. Repeat on the other end, substituting a chain for the clasp.

1 earrings • Cut a 6-in. (15 cm) piece of thread or braiding string. String: 11º seed bead, bicone crystal, 11º, round crystal, 11º, crystal rondelle, 11º, round, 11º, bicone, 11º. Center the beads.

2 Tie an overhand knot (Basics, p. 12) next to the first and last 11º.

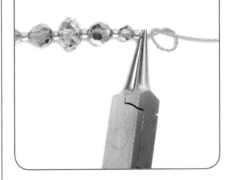

3 Trim the excess thread. Apply glue and string a crimp end over both ends. Flatten the crimp portion of the crimp end (Basics).

4 Open the loop of an earring wire (Basics) and attach the dangle. Close the loop. Make a second earring to match the first.

Supplies

necklace 19 in. (48 cm)

- 18–36 mm cubic zirconia (CZ) pendant
- **8–12** 8 mm crystal rondelles
- **16–24** 6 mm round crystals
- **16–24** 4 mm bicone crystals
- 2 g 11º seed beads
- 18–24 in. (46–61 cm) C-lon thread or braiding string
- **2** 4–6 mm jump rings
- **2** crimp ends
- lobster claw clasp
- 2 in. (5 cm) chain for extender, 2–3 mm links
- chainnose and roundnose pliers, or **2** pairs of chainnose pliers
- diagonal wire cutters
- adhesive

earrings

- **2** 8 mm crystal rondelles
- **4** 6 mm round crystals
- **4** 4 mm bicone crystals
- **12** 11º seed beads
- 12 in. (30 cm) C-lon thread or braiding string
- **2** crimp ends
- pair of earring wires
- chainnose and roundnose pliers, or **2** pairs of chainnose pliers
- diagonal wire cutters
- adhesive

Tip

Use the tip of your roundnose pliers to push the beads together as you tighten each knot.

Design alternative

For a more earthy option, try a neutral-toned gemstone pendant in place of the CZ pendant.

Linked
bracelets

Crystal links and tiny jump rings add up to a big, bold cuff

by Jean Yates

The chunky look of a cuff and the suppleness of chain come together in this bracelet. Two-loop crystal channels linked with oval jump rings form delicate lines, but this is no dainty design. Eight strands and three crystal squares create fullness and a wealth of sparkle. Three-strand earrings echo but don't overpower the glitz on your wrist.

1 bracelet • Open an oval jump ring (Basics, p. 12) and attach two color A channels. Close the jump ring. Use jump rings to make a seven-channel chain. Make eight color A and eight color B channel chains with seven channels each.

2 Use a 6–7 mm jump ring to attach four color A and four color B channel chains. Use a second 6–7 mm jump ring to attach the first jump ring and a single color A channel. Attach a third 6–7 mm jump ring and the other loop of the single channel.

3 String three square pendants over the single channel. Use a 6–7 mm jump ring to attach the channel's remaining jump ring and four color A and four color B channel chains.

4 On each end, use a 6–7 mm jump ring to attach the four color A channel chains and one loop of a two-strand clasp. Repeat to attach the color B channel chains to the other loop.

1 earrings • Follow step 1 of the bracelet to make one color A three-channel chain and two color B five-channel chains.

2 Use an oval jump ring to attach an end loop of each channel chain. Repeat on the other ends of the channel chains.

3 Open the loop of an earring wire (Basics, p. 12) and attach a jump ring from step 2. Close the loop. Make a second earring to match the first.

Supplies

bracelet
- **3** 20 mm square crystal pendants
- **113** 8 mm round double-loop crystal channels, **57** in color A, **56** in color B
- **8** 6–7 mm jump rings
- **96** 4–5 mm oval jump rings
- two-strand clasp
- chainnose and roundnose pliers, or **2** pairs of chainnose pliers

earrings
- **26** 8 mm round double-loop crystal channels, **6** in color A, **20** in color B
- **24** 4–5 mm oval jump rings pair of earring wires
- chainnose and roundnose pliers, or **2** pairs of chainnose pliers

Design alternative

Display a square pendant front and center by wrapping 22-gauge wire around its sides and through a pair of three-to-one-connectors. Make a simple loop on each end of the wire to keep it from poking your wrist.

Tip

If the single channel and jump ring from step 2 slip into the square pendants as you complete step 3, use a pin to anchor the jump ring to a piece of Styrofoam or corkboard.

"My favorite gemstone is pink sapphire, pink being one of my favorite colors. I never grew up! I haven't gotten past the pony stage yet."

Clear
winner

Beautiful blue hues meet in a sparkling design

by Cathy Jakicic

It's hard to pick a favorite color from the CRYSTALLIZED™ – *Swarovski Elements* rainbow, so why not choose the shade that goes with everything — crystal? In this necklace-and-earrings set, I used bicones in crystal, accented with Montana and tanzanite. The combination is sublime.

1 necklace • Cut three pieces of beading wire, each 38–48 in. (.97–1.2 m) long. On one wire, center a pendant.

2 On each end, string a 4 mm tanzanite bicone, a 6 mm Montana bicone, and a tanzanite. String 4 mm crystal bicones until the strand is within ½ in. (1.3 cm) of the finished length.

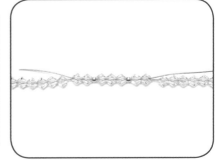

3 On one end, string a crimp bead, three crystal bicones, and a crimp bead. String the other end through the beads just strung, plus a few more. Tighten the wire and flatten the crimp beads (Basics, p. 12). Trim the excess wire.

4 On the second wire, string a tanzanite, a Montana, a tanzanite, and 13 crystal bicones. Repeat until the strand is within ½ in. (1.3 cm) of the finished length. Follow step 3 to finish the strand.

On the third wire, string crystal bicones until the strand is within ½ in. (1.3 cm) of the finished length Follow step 3 to finish the strand.

5 Looping one end of each strand over your index fingers, twist the strands together. Open a pearl shortener and attach the ends of the twisted strands.

"Is it possible to have a favorite Swarovski crystal color? There are so many to choose from and I love them all."
– BeadStyle survey response

1 earrings • On a head pin, string four 4 mm crystal bicones. Make the first half of a wrapped loop (Basics, p. 12). On a head pin, string a 4 mm tanzanite bicone and a 6 mm Montana bicone. Using the largest part of your roundnose pliers, make a plain loop (Basics).

2 Attach the four-crystal unit to the loop of an earring hoop. Complete the wraps.

3 String the two-crystal unit over the hoop. Make a second earring to match the first.

Design alternative

If you're looking for more color, combine Montana, tanzanite, and indicolite dangles on a simple chain for striking results.

Supplies

necklace (32 in./81 cm; with pearl shortener 14 in./36 cm)
- 30 mm avant-garde pendant, crystal
- **16–20** 6 mm bicone crystals, Montana
- **616–660** (5 gross) 4 mm bicone crystals, crystal
- **32–40** 4 mm bicone crystals, tanzanite
- flexible beading wire, .014 or .015
- pearl shortener
- **6** crimp beads
- chainnose pliers
- diagonal wire cutters

earrings
- **2** 6 mm bicone crystals, Montana
- **8** 4 mm bicone crystals, crystal
- **2** 4 mm bicone crystals, tanzanite
- **4** 1½-in. (3.8 cm) head pins pair of square earring hoops with one loop
- chainnose pliers
- roundnose pliers
- diagonal wire cutters

Tips

• Wear one or all of the necklace strands without the pearl shortener for a long, swingy look.
• Remove the Montana/tanzanite dangle from the earrings, and they'll match nearly everything in your wardrobe.
• To save money, buy large quantities of crystals from vendors that sell them by the gross.

Creative bent

Ornate gunmetal
connectors give
shape to retro style

by Irina Miech

Starburst ring

Ensnare crystals with well-placed wire wraps

by Elizabeth Perez

This ring is the perfect project for the wirework lover. Just a handful of loops creates the base for a mini explosion of crystal sparkle. A ring mandrel makes wrapping the ring base a snap, but you can use your finger in a pinch.

1 On a head pin, string a bead cap and a bicone crystal. Make the first half of a wrapped loop (Basics, p. 12). Make seven bicone units without bead caps. Complete the wraps.

2 Cut a 30-in. (76 cm) piece of wire. Starting 4 in. (10 cm) from one end, wrap it four times around your finger or a mandrel at the correct ring size. Bend the 4-in. tail up.

3 Remove the loops from the mandrel. Wrap the angled wire tail around the loops and trim the excess wire.

4 Use chainnose pliers to slightly raise a loop in the center of the ring base, near the wraps.

5 Attach the bead-cap unit to the raised part of the loop. Complete the wraps. Wrap the remaining wire once around the base of the bead-cap unit.

6 String the bicone units on the wire surrounding the bead cap unit. Wrap the wire around the base of the units until there is about 4 in. (10 cm) remaining.

7 Wrap the wire around the ring-base loops and trim the excess wire.

Tip

If you're using a mix of colors, arrange the bicone units so the colors are evenly spaced.

Supplies

- **8** 6 mm bicone crystals
- 6 mm bead cap
- 30 in. (76 cm) 22-gauge half-hard wire
- **8** 1½-in. (3.8 cm) head pins
- chainnose and roundnose pliers
- diagonal wire cutters
- ring mandrel (optional)

Design alternative

Colorful Artistic Wire and one "avant-garde" crystal transform a sweetly old-fashioned look into modern art.

❝I love bold rings with a lot of sparkle. Wire and crystals are my favorite materials.**❞**

Pretty in paisley

Nestle sparkling crystals in unusual chain

by Rebekah Gough

The curvy links of this paisley chain are a perfect place to add a little sparkle. Simple wire wraps do the job nicely, making this a great project for a novice wireworker. Snip a few extra links for some quick matching earrings.

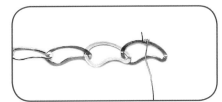

1 **a** bracelet • Cut a 7–8-in. (18–20 cm) piece of chain.
b Cut a 2½-in. (6.4 cm) piece of wire. Wrap the wire around one side of a link three times.

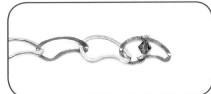

2 **a** String a bicone crystal on the wire. Wrap the wire around the other side of the link three times. Trim the excess wire. Use chainnose pliers to flatten the wire against the link.
b Repeat steps 1b and 2a for each link.

Supplies

bracelet
- **14–16** 4–6 mm bicone crystals
- 35–40 in. (89–102 cm) 26-gauge dead-soft wire
- 7–8 in. (18–20 cm) paisley chain
- lobster claw clasp
- chainnose and roundnose pliers
- diagonal wire cutters

earrings
- **4** 6 mm bicone crystals
- **4** 4 mm bicone crystals
- 20 in. (51 cm) 26-gauge dead-soft wire
- 4 in. (10 cm) paisley chain
- **2** 6 mm jump rings
- pair of earring wires
- chainnose and roundnose pliers, or **2** pairs of chainnose pliers
- diagonal wire cutters

3 Cut a 2½-in. (6.4 cm) piece of wire. Make the first half of a wrapped loop (Basics, p. 12). String a bicone and make the first half of a wrapped loop.

4 Attach the chain and a lobster claw clasp to each loop of the bicone unit and complete the wraps.

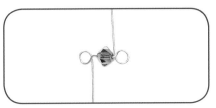

1 earrings • Cut a link of chain. Following bracelet steps 1b and 2a, attach a 6 mm and a 4 mm bicone crystal. Repeat with a second link.

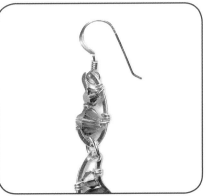

2 Open a jump ring (Basics, p. 12). Attach the links and close the jump ring. Open the loop of an earring wire (Basics), attach the dangle, and close the loop. Make a second earring to match the first.

Tips

• To commemorate a birthday, substitute tiny gemstones for the bicone crystals.
• To create a personalized gift for a mom, use bicones that represent her kids' birthdays.

Simple sparklers

Swarovski crystal-studded beads shine in a pair of earrings

by Maria Camera

String these light-catching beauties with just a bicone crystal or two, and this stunningly simple design yields a simply stunning pair of earrings.

Supplies

- **2** 14 mm Swarovski crystal-studded beads
- **4** 4 mm bicone crystals
- **2** 2-in. (5 cm) head pins
- pair of earring wires
- chainnose and roundnose pliers
- diagonal wire cutters

1 On a head pin, string a bicone crystal, a crystal-studded bead, and a bicone. Make a plain loop (Basics, p. 12).

2 Open the loop of an earring wire (Basics). Attach the dangle and close the loop. Make a second earring to match the first.

Tip

Can't stop at just one crystal-studded bead? String beads in different colors on the same head pin for an ultra-glamorous set of dangles.

Stack of sparkle

Transform a piece of wire and a couple of crystals into a fabulous ring

by Karla Schafer

You'll love the brilliance of a crystal rondelle perched upon a square pendant, but this ring is open to creative interpretation. Just make sure both beads have holes large enough to accommodate two ends of 20-gauge wire. If you're already an expert in wire-wrapping, try this project with 18-gauge wire.

This ring showcases beads in crystal copper and crystal volcano.

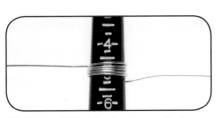

1 Cut a 3-ft. (.9 m) piece of wire. Place the wire against a ring mandrel at the desired size. Wrap it around five or six times.

2 Bring the two ends together. Over both ends, string a square pendant and a crystal rondelle.

3 Use your fingers to gently coil the pair of wires around the rondelle. Separate the wires so they point in opposite directions.

4 Wrap each wire around the band five or six times. Trim the excess wire. Use chainnose or crimping pliers to tuck each end.

5 To tighten the wraps, place the ring on the mandrel. Gently push the ring band down the mandrel.

Design alternatives

Consider plastic and Lucite beads for fun rings. They tend to have large holes that can accommodate 20-gauge wire. Or, for a cocktail ring, try stacking a rondelle and a square on top of a 30 mm square.

Supplies

- ◆ 14 mm square crystal pendant
- ◆ 12 mm crystal rondelle
- ◆ 3 ft. (.9 m) 20-gauge Artistic Wire
- ◆ chainnose or crimping pliers
- ◆ diagonal wire cutters
- ◆ ring mandrel

A STRAIGHT line

Create a dazzling lariat shimmering with crystals

by Erin Dolan

While short, chunky styles add bulk, a lariat lengthens and adds height. Make an extra-long necklace that sparkles from your neck to your waist.

❝A long necklace creates a lean line that gives the illusion of height.❞

1 On a head pin, string a crystal. Make a plain loop (Basics, p. 12). Make 90 to 110 crystal units.

2 Decide how long you want your lariat to be and cut a piece of chain to that length. Open the loop of a crystal unit (Basics) and attach it to the center link of the chain. Close the loop. Attach six to eight more crystal units to the center link.

3 On each side of the center link, skip five links and attach three crystal units to the next link. Continue attaching crystal units, leaving five links open between each cluster. Leave the last 10 to 15 links open on each end.

4 On each end, attach a total of six to 10 crystal units to the last three chain links.

Supplies

lariat 60 in. (1.5 m)

- **90–110** 3–8 mm assorted crystals
- **4–5** ft. (1.2–1.5 m) chain, 10–12 mm links
- **90–110** 2-in. (5 cm) 22-gauge head pins
- chainnose and roundnose pliers
- diagonal wire cutters

Design alternative

String crystals and seed beads on beading wire for a shorter, less time-consuming lariat. For a 32-in. (81 cm) lariat, you'll need 100 to 125 crystals.

Tips

- Make your plain loops large enough so they can easily fit around the chain links.
- If your loops are too small or if you want a more uniform lariat, attach the crystal units in each cluster to a jump ring. Then, attach the jump ring to the chain link.
- The lariat's length makes it a versatile piece. Fold it in half and slide both ends through the fold, or loop the ends in a loose knot.

Metal

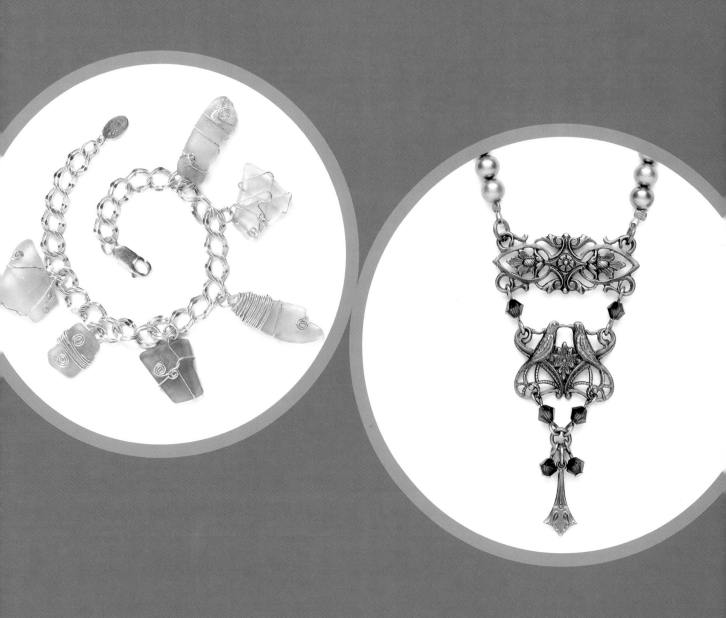

and chain

Filigree findings and crystals
make a gift-worthy necklace
and earrings

by **Monica Lueder**

Wrap up a
vintage
look

I'm a jewelry hound. I love big, bold pieces and anything vintage. With these filigree findings, I transformed modern cabochons into a pendant that looks antique. It's an instant heirloom that's sure to be treasured. Experiment with different filigrees and cabochons (see the design alternative) to create your own ornate look.

1 necklace • With diagonal wire cutters, trim the center from a filigree to accommodate an 18 mm cabochon. Use chainnose pliers to bend the filigree around a 35 mm cabochon. Glue the small cabochon to the center of the large one.

2 On an eye pin, string a bead cap, a round crystal, and a bead cap. Make a plain loop (Basics, p. 12). Make eight to 10 round-crystal units.

On an eye pin, string a bicone crystal and make a plain loop perpendicular to the first loop. Make 10 to 12 bicone units.

3 Cut 16 to 18 ¼–½-in. (6–13 mm) pieces of chain.

Open a loop (Basics) of a bicone unit. Attach a chain and close the loop. Attach the other end of the chain, one loop of a round-crystal unit, and another chain. Repeat.

4 Open a jump ring (Basics). Attach one side of the pendant and the other loop of the bicone unit. Close the jump ring. Repeat on the other side. Continue attaching bead units and chains until the strand is within ½ in. (1.3 cm) of the finished length. End with a chain.

5 On one end, use a jump ring to attach a lobster claw clasp. Repeat on the other end, substituting a soldered jump ring for the clasp.

Tip

Try trimming different filigree shapes to see what best suits the cabochon you're using.

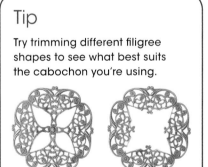

93

1 earrings • On an eye pin, string a round crystal and make a plain loop (Basics, p. 12). On another eye pin, string a bicone crystal, a rondelle, and a bicone. Make a plain loop perpendicular to the first loop.

2 Cut a two-link piece of chain. Open a jump ring (Basics) and attach a filigree. Close the jump ring.

3 Open each loop (Basics) of the round-crystal unit. Attach the filigree dangle on one end and the rondelle unit on the other. Close the loops.

4 Open the loop of an earring wire. Attach the dangle and close the loop. Make a second earring to match the first.

Supplies

necklace 16½ in. (41.9 cm)

- 35 mm cabochon
- 18 mm cabochon
- **8–10** 10 mm round crystals
- **10–12** 6 mm bicone crystals
- **16–20** 10 mm bead caps
- 6–11 in. (15–28 cm) chain, 3–4 mm links
- 47 mm filigree
- **18–22** 1½-in. (3.8 cm) eye pins
- **3** 5 mm jump rings
- lobster claw clasp and soldered jump ring
- chainnose and roundnose pliers
- diagonal wire cutters
- Super New Glue

earrings

- **2** 8 mm round crystals
- **2** 5 mm crystal-accent rondelles
- **4** 4 mm bicone crystals
- **1** in. (2.5 cm) chain, 3–4 mm links
- **2** 33 mm teardrop filigrees
- **4** 1½-in. (3.8 cm) eye pins
- **2** 4–5 mm jump rings
- pair of earring wires
- chainnose and roundnose pliers
- diagonal wire cutters

Design alternative

For a pieces with holiday hues, try a red faceted glass centerpiece and add garnet-colored dangles.

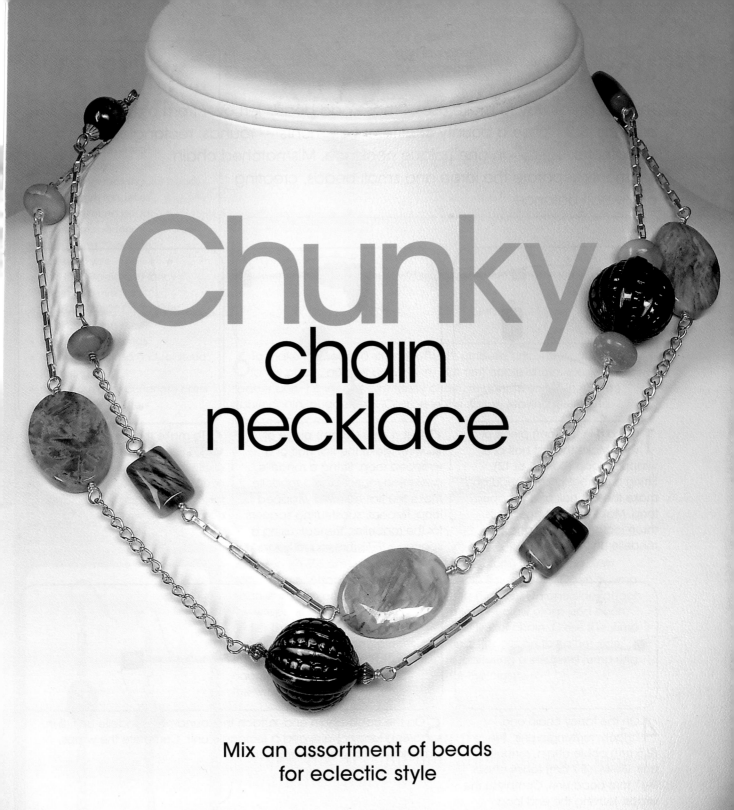

Chunky
chain
necklace

**Mix an assortment of beads
for eclectic style**

by Lacy Halliwell

Empowerment by DeZine

Select handmade brass and silver components from Africa

by Jane Konkel

DeZine is a small factory in South Africa that employs mostly women, many of whom are physically challenged. As supporters of the Black Economic Empowerment Act, DeZine pays fair wages and helps employees learn life skills, such as finances, computer literacy, birth control, and disease prevention. In compliance with the act, companies buy products from other African vendors to ensure economic empowerment in South Africa. One example: these handmade brass and silver components, enameled and coated with antitarnish lacquer.

Supplies

necklace 14 in. (36 cm)
- 40 x 50 mm enamel pendant, with two holes
- **2** 10 mm jump rings
- 2 piece 4½–6 in. (11.4–15 cm) neckwire
- chainnose and round-nose pliers, or **2** pairs of chainnose pliers

earrings
- **2** 25 x 30 mm enamel pendants, with two holes
- **4** 4 mm spacers
- 6 in. (15 cm) 18-gauge half-hard wire
- **8** 5 mm jump rings
- pair of earring wires

- chainnose and roundnose pliers
- diagonal wire cutters

Supplies shown from Antelope Beads, antelopebeads.com.

necklace • Open a jump ring (Basics, p. 12). Attach a loop of the neckwire and a hole of the pendant. Close the jump ring. Use a jump ring to attach the other loop and hole.

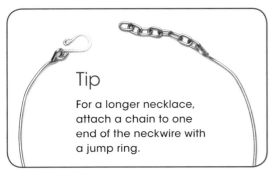

Tip

For a longer necklace, attach a chain to one end of the neckwire with a jump ring.

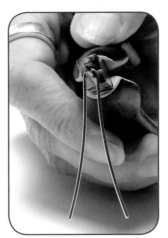

1 **earrings •** Cut a 3-in (7.6 cm) piece of wire. Use roundnose pliers to bend the wire in half.

2 On each end of the wire, string a spacer and make a plain loop (Basics, p. 12).

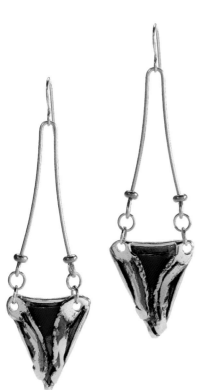

3 Open a jump ring (Basics) and attach a plain loop. Close the jump ring. Use a jump ring to attach a hole of a pendant. Repeat with the remaining hole.

4 Open the loop of an earring wire (Basics). Attach the dangle and close the loop. Make a second earring to match the first.

Wired
herringbone
bracelet

Weave and wire away to connect these shapely stones

by Mia Gofar

You might think a faceted gemstone rondelle or a round bead nested in a wire herringbone frame looks awesome but is difficult to make. You're half right. Though this project has many steps, it's really straightforward. You'll have a gorgeous bracelet in no time.

Supplies

- **3–4** 22–28 mm gemstone nuggets
- **2–3** 10–12 mm rondelles or round beads
- 48–72 in. (1.2–1.8 m) 22-gauge half-hard wire
- 34–41 in. (.86–1 m) 20-gauge half-hard wire
- hook-and-eye clasp
- chainnose and roundnose pliers
- diagonal wire cutters

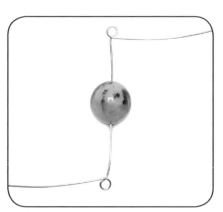

1 To make a herringbone unit: Cut a 7-in. (18 cm) piece of 20-gauge wire. Center a 10–12 mm bead. On each side, ½ in. (1.3 cm) from the bead, make the first half of a wrapped loop (Basics, p. 12).

2 Complete the wraps. Make the same number of coils on each side of the bead.

3 Cut a 24-in. (61 cm) piece of 22-gauge wire. Wrap one end around the coils twice at the base of the bead. Trim the excess wire.

4 Wrap the working wire around the bead, taking it in front of and around the bottom coils once.

5 Wrap the wire around the bead, taking it in front of and around the top coils once.

6 Repeat steps 4 and 5 until you can no longer wrap. Wrap the wire twice just below the top loop. Trim the excess wire.

Make two or three herringbone bead units.

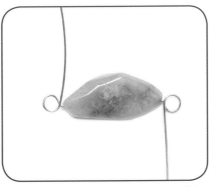

7 To make a bead unit: Cut a 5-in. (13 cm) piece of 20-gauge wire. Make the first half of a wrapped loop. String a nugget and make the first half of a wrapped loop. Make four nugget units.

8 Attach a loop of a nugget unit and half of a clasp. Complete the wraps. Attach the remaining loop and a herringbone unit. As you complete the wraps, coil the wire end over the nugget.

Attach the remaining nugget units and herringbone units. Attach the remaining clasp half.

Customize a cuff

Embellished bracelets make for up-to-the-minute fashion
by Rupa Balachandar

Cuff-style bracelets are all the rage. Add a glamorous spin to yours with crystals, gemstones, rhinestones, and filigree. The hinged version is a ritzy option if you have wider wrists.

1 cuff bracelet • Use your fingers to flatten the edges of the filigree. Apply a thin coating of adhesive to the back of the filigree and to the center of the cuff. Allow to dry for 5 minutes. Press the surfaces together. Allow to dry completely.

2 Glue a 12 mm flat-bottom crystal to the center of the filigree as in step 1.

3 Glue a cupped rhinestone to each of the four corners of the filigree as in step 1.

1 hinged bracelet • Glue three flat-back crystals to one side of a hinged bracelet as in step 1 of the cuff bracelet.

2 Glue a filigree with flower and the remaining flat-back crystals to the other side of the bracelet as in step 1 of the cuff bracelet.

Supplies

cuff bracelet
- 55 mm filigree
- 12 mm flat-bottom crystal
- **4** 6 mm cupped rhinestones
- 35 mm gold-plated cuff
- E6000 adhesive

hinged bracelet
- 28 mm filigree with crystal flower
- **5** 7 mm flat-back crystals
- 27 mm gold-plated hinged bracelet
- E6000 adhesive

earrings
- **2** 28 mm filigree with crystal flowers
- **2** 9 mm triangular crystal charms
- **2** 4 mm jump rings
- pair of lever-back earring wires
- chainnose and roundnose pliers, or **2** pairs of chainnose pliers

1 earrings • Open a jump ring (Basics, p. 12) and attach a triangular charm and a filigree with flower. Close the jump ring.

2 Open the loop of an earring wire (Basics) and attach the dangle. Close the loop. Make a second earring to match the first.

Design alternative

For this bracelet, I glued an epoxy typewriter key in a cabochon setting then glued the setting to the filigree. The epoxy typewriter key and 18 mm round cabochon setting are from Ornamentea, ornamentea.com.

Antique
treasures

Connect filigrees for a vintage-style
necklace and earrings

by Irina Miech

To make a necklace that celebrates
the lavish and geometric feel of Art Deco
design, I created a tapered pendant by
connecting three different filigree shapes
with crystal bead units. Bronze pearls
match the patina on brass filigrees. The
repeated motif in simple earrings extends
the opulence.

1 necklace • On a head pin,
string a bicone crystal. Make a
plain loop (Basics, p. 12). Make a
second head-pin unit. On an eye
pin, string a bicone. Make a plain
loop. Make four eye-pin units.

2 Open a jump ring (Basics).
Attach a filigree charm and
close the jump ring. Use a
second jump ring to attach a
head-pin unit, the charm unit,
and a head-pin unit.

3 Open the loops of an eye-pin
unit (Basics). Attach one corner
of a 20 mm filigree and the dangle
from step 2. Close the loops.
Repeat on the adjacent corner
of the filigree.

4 Use eye-pin units to attach the remaining corners of the 20 mm filigree and two corners of a 30 mm filigree. Attach a jump ring to each remaining corner of the 30 mm filigree.

5 Cut two 7–8-in. (18–20 cm) pieces of beading wire. On one end of each wire, string a crimp bead and one of the pendant's jump rings. Go back through the crimp bead and tighten the wire. Crimp the crimp bead (Basics).

6 On each end, string pearls until the strand is within 1 in. (2.5 cm) of the finished length. String a crimp bead and half of a clasp. Check the fit, and add or remove beads if necessary. Go back through the last few beads strung and tighten the wire. Crimp the crimp bead and trim the excess wire.

1 earrings • On an eye pin, string a bicone crystal. Make a plain loop (Basics, p. 12) perpendicular to the other loop.

2 Open one loop (Basics) and attach a filigree charm. Close the loop.

3 Open the loop of an earring wire and attach the dangle. Close the loop. Make a second earring to match the first.

Supplies

necklace 18½ in. (47 cm)
- 16-in. (41 cm) strand 4–5 mm pearls
- **6** 4 mm bicone crystals
- flexible beading wire, .014 or .015
- 30 mm filigree
- 20 mm filigree
- 14 mm filigree charm
- **2** 1-in. (2.5 cm) head pins
- **4** 1-in. (2.5 cm) eye pins
- **4** 4 mm jump rings
- **4** crimp beads
- hook-and-eye clasp
- chainnose and roundnose pliers
- diagonal wire cutters
- crimping pliers (optional)

earrings
- **2** 14 mm filigree charms
- **2** 4 mm bicone crystals
- **2** 1-in. (2.5 cm) eye pins
- pair of earring wires
- chainnose and roundnose pliers
- diagonal wire cutters

Design alternative

For a pop of color in the pendant, sandwich a 14 mm rivoli stone between two 20 mm square filigrees. Attach the filigrees with jump rings and add crystal dangles in a matching color.

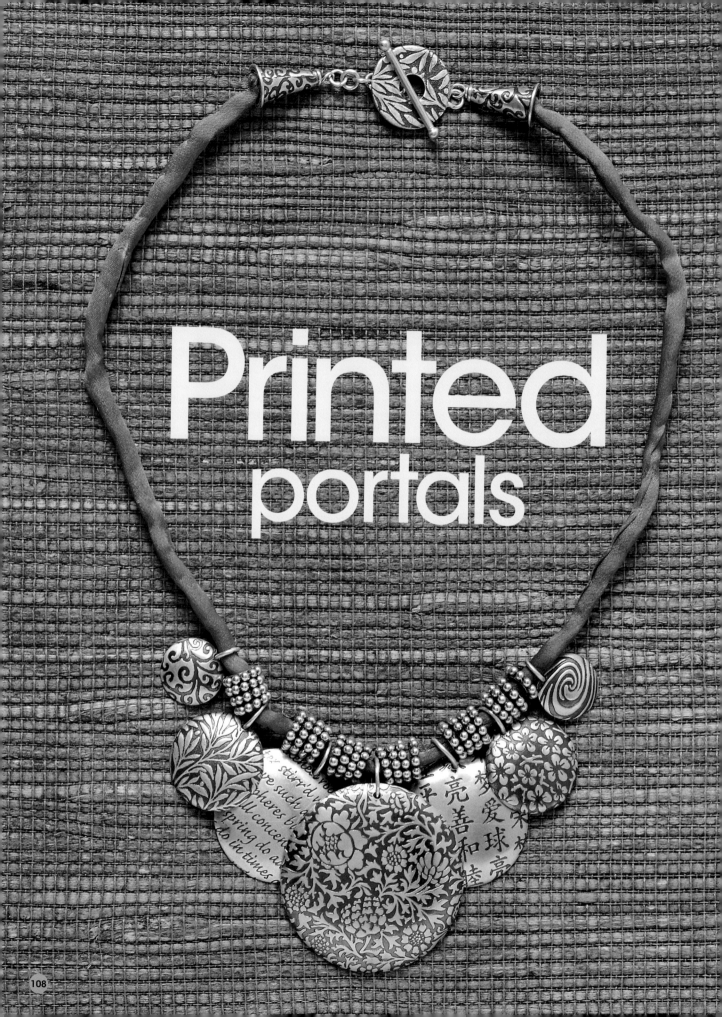

Printed
portals

Sample a parade of pendants

by Nina Cooper

To show off these pendants, I had a vision of a layered collar with juxtaposed textures. I designed this necklace to feature a cascade of round pendants handmade in Bali silver. The pendants provide a glimpse of Japanese plum blossoms and flowery English poetry, Chinese text and a swirling pool.

1 **necklace** • Cut a 20–24-in. (51–61 cm) piece of silk cord. Center: 24 mm pendant, three or four spacers, 40 mm pendant, three or four spacers, 24 mm pendant.

2 On each end, string three or four spacers, an 18 mm pendant, three or four spacers, and a 12 mm pendant.

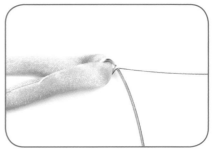

3 Cut a 4-in. (10 cm) piece of wire. Make the first half of a wrapped loop (Basics, p. 12) 1 in. (2.5 cm) from one end. String one end of the cord and fold it, leaving a ½-in. (1.3 cm) tail. Complete the wraps, wrapping the wire tightly around the folded cord. Trim the excess wire and tuck the end under the wraps. Repeat on the other end of the cord. Trim the excess cord.

❝When designing this necklace, I wanted it to create unity from bits and pieces of other times and places.❞

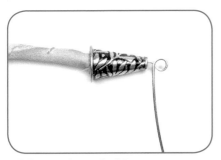

4 On each end, string a cone and make the first half of a wrapped loop.

5 On each end, attach half of a clasp and complete the wraps.

Tip

If you are layering pendants, it helps to alternate between busy and simple patterns.

1 earrings · On a decorative head pin, string an oval bead and make the first half of a wrapped loop (Basics, p. 12).

2 Attach a spacer and complete the wraps.

3 Open a jump ring (Basics) and attach the dangle and the loop of an earring wire. Close the jump ring. Make a second earring to match the first.

Supplies

necklace 16 in. (41 cm)
- 40 mm extra-large disk pendant
- **2** 24 mm round domed pendants
- **2** 18 mm round domed pendants
- **2** 12 mm round domed pendants
- **18–24** 9 mm large-hole flat spacers
- 20–24 in. (51–61 cm) silk cord, 3 mm wide
- 8 in. (20 cm) 22-gauge dead-soft wire
- **2** 13 mm small cones
- toggle clasp
- chainnose and roundnose pliers
- diagonal wire cutters

earrings
- **2** 12 mm oval beads
- **2** 9 mm large-hole flat spacers
- **2** 2-in. (5 cm) decorative head pins
- **2** 5 mm jump rings
- pair of decorative earring wires
- chainnose and roundnose pliers
- diagonal wire cutters

Supplies from Nina Designs, ninadesigns.com. All pendants have jump rings attached.

Design alternative

For a budget-friendly necklace, use just three small silver pendants, or hang brass pendants from leather cord. Brass pendants from Jewels n Findings, jewelsnfindings.com.

Around the BEND

Make pretty earrings with a quick curve of wire

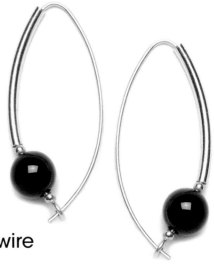

by Jess DiMeo

These fun earrings take just minutes to make — perfect for an easy gift. Try different tube and bead sizes for styles that suit everyone on your list.

Supplies

- **2** 1-in. (2.5 cm) curved silver tube beads
- **2** 8 mm round beads
- **4** 2–3 mm round spacers
- 8 in. (20 cm) 20-gauge half-hard wire
- chainnose and roundnose pliers
- diagonal wire cutters
- metal file or emery board

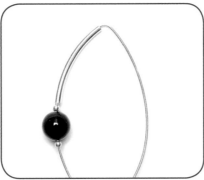

1 Cut a 4-in. (10 cm) piece of wire. Bend it in half. On one end, string a curved-tube bead, a spacer, an 8 mm bead, and a spacer.

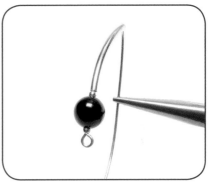

2 Make a plain loop (Basics, p. 12). File the other end of the wire. Make a second earring to match the first.

Tips

- Leave a small space between the tube and the bend so the tube doesn't poke your ear.
- For a mixed-metal look that goes with everything, use gold-filled wire with sterling silver tubes, or vice versa.

66 Our customers were my inspiration for these earrings. Our approach is to always try to keep gorgeous jewelry affordable. 99

Design alternative

For a sister or friend who likes dressier earrings, try gold tube beads with filigree rounds and 12 mm crystal pearls.

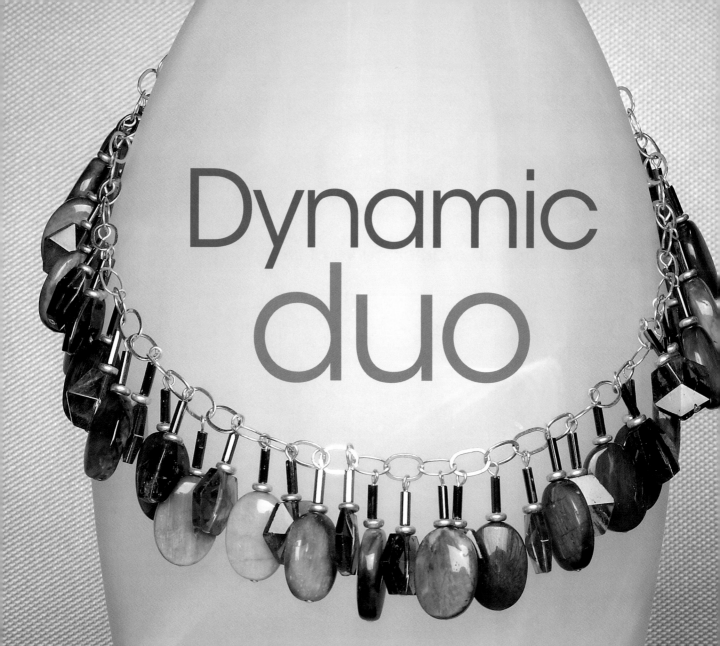

Dynamic duo

Pair ovals and hexagons to make a
handsome necklace

by Monica Lueder

This necklace is a great way to practice making simple plain loops. I used 18 mm oval beads and 13 mm hexagons, but just about any similarly sized combination will yield attractive results. Use large-link chain that gives the beads room to move.

1 On a head pin, string an oval bead, a spacer, and a bugle bead. Make a plain loop (Basics, p. 12). Make 23 to 29 oval-bead units and 22 to 28 hexagon-bead units.

2 Decide how long you want your necklace to be and cut a piece of chain to that length. Open the loop of an oval-bead unit (Basics) and attach it to the center link. Close the loop. On each side, attach alternating hexagon and oval-bead units.

3 Check the fit, and trim chain from each end if necessary. On one end, open a jump ring (Basics) and attach a lobster claw clasp. Close the jump ring.

Supplies

necklace 16½ in. (41.9 cm)

- 16-in. (41 cm) strand 18 mm oval beads
- 16-in. (41 cm) strand 13 mm hexagon beads
- **45–57** 6 mm bugle beads
- **45–57** 4 mm spacers
- 15–17 in. (38–43 cm) chain, 8–10 mm links
- **45–57** 2-in. (5 cm) head pins
- 5 mm jump ring
- lobster claw clasp
- chainnose and roundnose pliers
- diagonal wire cutters

Design alternative

This extra-long version is perfect for turtlenecks in winter. Though this design uses just one gemstone shape, two types of seed beads provide a subtle contrast.

Tip

If you use 12 mm or smaller gemstones, 1½-in. (3.8 cm) head pins should be long enough.

66My style changes all the time. I get excited about the smallest details.99

Snare treasures from the sea

Encircle sea glass with wrapped wire

by Christine Haynes

A friend of mine collects sea glass. When she came to me with these pretty little pieces, I could see they were very special to her — she even remembered where and when she picked them up! The wire wraps in this charm bracelet are the perfect way for her to keep her sea treasures close, and we continue to add new pieces as her collection grows.

Supplies

- **6** pieces of sea glass
- 5 ft. (1.5 m) 24-gauge half-hard wire
- 7–9 in. (18–23 cm) chain, 8–10 mm links
- **8** 4–5 mm jump rings
- lobster claw clasp and soldered jump ring
- chainnose and roundnose pliers
- diagonal wire cutters
- G-S Hypo Cement

Sea glass

Sea glass is formed when bottles, tableware, and other glass objects make their way into lakes and oceans and are tumbled smooth by the water and sand. You can find authentic sea glass on the beach or purchase it from collectors on eBay.com. You can buy artificial sea glass at your local craft store.

  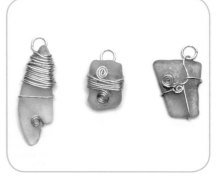

1 Cut a 10-in. (25 cm) piece of wire and make a 4 mm spiral on one end (Spiral, below). Press the spiral to a piece of sea glass and wrap the wire around the back. Glue the spiral to the sea glass and let dry.

2 Wrap the wire around the sea glass as desired. Toward the top of the sea glass, on the back side, make a loop and continue wrapping. Open a jump ring (Basics, p. 12) and attach the loop. Close the jump ring.

3 When you're finished wrapping, glue the wire end to the wraps on the back of the sea glass. Alternatively, make a spiral and glue it to the front of the sea glass, or make a spiral and hook it around a wrap. Repeat steps 1–3 with the remaining sea glass.

4 Decide how long you want your bracelet to be, and cut a piece of chain to that length. Open the jump ring on a piece of sea glass and attach a link 1½ in. (3.8 cm) from the end of the chain. Close the jump ring. Continue attaching sea glass every three or four links.

5 On one end of the chain, use a jump ring to attach a lobster claw clasp. Repeat on the other end, substituting a soldered jump ring for the clasp.

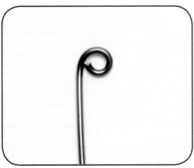  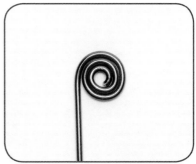

Spiral

1. Grasp the end of the wire with the tip of your roundnose pliers. Rotate the pliers to form a loop. If the start of the loop is straight rather than rounded, trim it off and rotate the wire again.

2. Grasp the loop horizontally with chainnose pliers so that just the edge of the loop is visible. Press the next ⅛ in. (3 mm) of the wire tail against the loop.

3. Reposition the pliers and press the next ⅛ in. (3 mm) of the wire tail against the loop. Repeat until the spiral is the desired size.

Wrap wire
by heart

This necklace makes a romantic accessory any time of year

by Christine Haynes

Button pearls in sweet shades lend a classic look, while the off-center heart pendant adds a modern edge. As a bonus, you get to practice basic wire wrapping. Once you've coiled your way around this heart, you'll be ready to wire-wrap just about any shape that crosses your path.

Supplies

necklace 16 in. (41 cm)
- 16-in. (41 cm) strand 4–5 mm button pearls
- flexible beading wire, .010 or .012
- 2½ in. (6.4 cm) 18-gauge wire
- 23 in. (58 cm) 24-gauge wire
- 6–7 mm jump ring
- **2** 2–3 mm jump rings
- **2** 4–5 mm split rings

- **2** crimp beads
- **2** crimp covers
- lobster claw clasp
- 2½ in. (6.4 cm) chain for extender, 3–5 mm links
- chainnose and roundnose pliers
- diagonal wire cutters
- crimping pliers (optional)
- split-ring pliers (optional)

1 Cut a 2½-in. (6.4 cm) piece of 18-gauge wire and bend it in half. On each end, make half of a loop using the largest part of your roundnose pliers. Use your fingers to form a heart shape.

2 Cut a 23-in. (58 cm) piece of 24-gauge wire and bend it in half. Place the bottom of the heart in the bend, and wrap the 24-gauge wire around each half of the heart, stringing button pearls as desired. Trim the excess wire and tuck the ends.

3 Open a 6–7 mm jump ring (Basics, p. 12) and attach the heart. Close the jump ring.

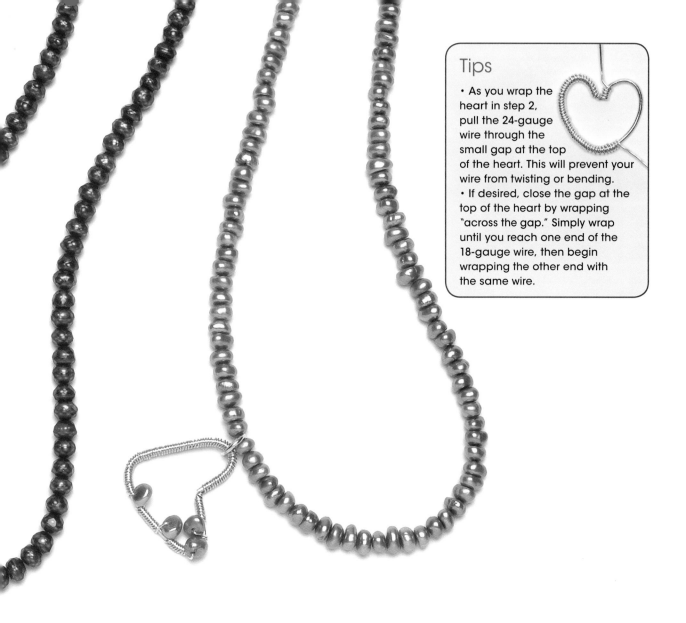

Tips

• As you wrap the heart in step 2, pull the 24-gauge wire through the small gap at the top of the heart. This will prevent your wire from twisting or bending.

• If desired, close the gap at the top of the heart by wrapping "across the gap." Simply wrap until you reach one end of the 18-gauge wire, then begin wrapping the other end with the same wire.

4 Cut a piece of beading wire (Basics) and string 6 in. (15 cm) of pearls and the heart pendant. String pearls until the strand is within 1 in. (2.5 cm) of the finished length.

5 On each end, string a crimp bead, a pearl, and a split ring. Check the fit, and add or remove pearls if necessary. Go back through the last few beads strung and tighten the wire. Crimp the crimp bead (Basics) and trim the excess wire.

6 On one end, use a 2–3 mm jump ring to attach a lobster claw clasp and the split ring. Repeat on the other end, substituting a 2½-in. (6.4 cm) piece of chain for the clasp. Close crimp covers over the crimps.

MiX iT UP WiTH

This brass pendant is a *melong.* Tibetan ritual items like this mirror are used by lamas, astrologers, and shamans. Design around a grand focal piece by incorporating copper and brass rondelles, or string a single type of metal. Whether you dress up the disk with kindred metals or mix things up a bit, your necklace will shine.

METAL

A disk pendant offers multiple design opportunities

by Helene Tsigistras

1 necklace • Cut a piece of beading wire (Basics, p. 12). Center a Wire Guardian and a pendant on the wire. Over both ends, string a metal rondelle. On each end, string a 4 mm rondelle.

2 On each end, string a metal tube bead, a metal rondelle, a nugget, and a metal rondelle.

3a On each end, string a metal tube bead. Alternate five metal rondelles with four 4 mm rondelles.
  b Repeat steps 2 and 3a. String a tube and a metal rondelle. Alternate metal rondelles with 4 mm rondelles until the strand is within 1 in. (2.5 cm) of the finished length.

4 On each end, string: 4 mm rondelle, crimp bead, 3 mm spacer, Wire Guardian, half of a clasp. Check the fit, and add or remove beads from each end if necessary. Go back through the beads just strung and tighten the wire. Crimp the crimp bead (Basics) and trim the excess wire.

Tip

Experiment with shapes. It's not necessary that the rondelles match. I used four different types of 10 mm brass rondelles in this necklace.

1 earrings • On a head pin, string: 4 mm rondelle, metal rondelle, 4 mm, metal, 4 mm. Make a plain loop (Basics, p. 12).

2 Open the loop of an earring wire (Basics) and attach the dangle. Close the loop. Make a second earring to match the first.

Design alternatives

I found this copper pendant at the *Bead&Button* Show. It reminds me of a tin ceiling tile. To keep the focus on the pendant's intricate details, I strung a backdrop of copper rondelles.

These very different metal pendants offer a range of exotic looks.

Supplies

necklace 22 in. (56 cm)
- 50–60 mm disk pendant (Tibetan Spirit, tibetanspirit.com)
- **10** 18–22 mm metal tube beads
- **4** 15–20 mm gemstone nuggets
- **31–35** 10 mm metal rondelles, **23–25** in brass, **8–10** in copper
- **18–20** 4 mm gemstone rondelles
- **2** 3 mm spacers
- flexible beading wire, .014 or .015
- **2** crimp beads
- **3** Wire Guardians
- toggle clasp
- chainnose or crimping pliers
- diagonal wire cutters

earrings
- **4** 10 mm metal rondelles
- **6** 4 mm gemstone rondelles
- **2** 1½-in. (3.8 cm) decorative head pins
- pair of earring wires
- chainnose and roundnose pliers
- diagonal wire cutters

Intricate
drops

Speed through a pair of filigree earrings

by Lauren Hadley

Grab a pair of gemstone briolettes and two filigrees, then bend a filigree around each stone. Make a wire-wrapped hanger and ta-da! A pair of gorgeous handmade earrings, as easy as 1–2–3.

1 Use chainnose pliers to bend the edges of a filigree around a briolette.

2 Cut a 6-in. (15 cm) piece of wire. String a filigree-wrapped briolette and make a set of wraps above it (Basics, p. 12). Make a wrapped loop (Basics).

3 Open the loop of an earring wire (Basics). Attach the dangle and close the loop. Make a second earring to match the first.

Supplies

- **2** 20–24 mm briolettes
- **2** 40 mm filigree connectors
- 12 in. (30 cm) 24-gauge half-hard wire
- pair of earring wires
- chainnose and roundnose pliers
- diagonal wire cutters

Fleur de lis filigree from Jewels n Findings, jewelsnfindings.com.

Suspended
briolette

Dangle a drop of color in the center of a wire pendant

by Tamira Williams

Beautiful briolettes are often sold singly, making this project the perfect place to showcase them. Use silver wire to match the cool colors of the season, or warm up with glowing gold. But have no fear for the safety of your stone — tiny wraps keep it suspended without the suspense.

1 Cut a 1½-in. (3.8 cm) piece of 22-gauge wire and make a plain loop (Basics, p. 12) on one end. String a bicone crystal and make a plain loop. Make a second bicone unit. Set aside for step 6.

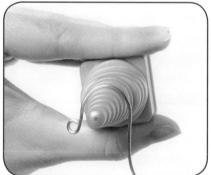

2 Cut a 7½-in. (19.1 cm) piece of 16-gauge wire. Make a loop on each end. With the loops facing up, wrap one end of the wire halfway around a mandrel or small round object, such as a pen. Repeat on the other end of the wire.

3 Center the mandrel and pull the ends of the wire together to form an open teardrop shape.

4 Cut a 4-in. (10 cm) piece of 22-gauge wire and center a briolette. Wrap one end of the wire around one side of the teardrop, just below the opening. Make four wraps. Trim the wire and tuck the end. Repeat on the other side.

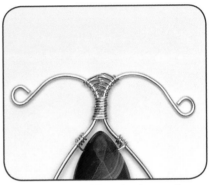

5 Cut a 7-in. (15 cm) piece of 22-gauge wire. Wrap the wire around the teardrop six to nine times to close it.

Wrap once around one side of the teardrop, then around the other side in the opposite direction. Make five or six figure-8 wraps. Trim the wire and tuck the end.

6 Cut two 8-10-in. (20-25 cm) pieces of chain. On each side, open the loops (Basics) of a bicone unit. Attach one loop to one side of the pendant and the other loop to a chain. Close the loops.

7 Open a jump ring (Basics) and attach an end link of chain and a lobster claw clasp. Repeat on the other side, substituting a soldered jump ring for the clasp.

Supplies

necklace 22 in. (56 cm)

- 16–23 mm gemstone briolette
- **2** 6 mm bicone crystals
- 7½ in. (19.1 cm) 16-gauge half-hard wire
- 14 in. (36 cm) 22-gauge half-hard wire
- 16–20 in. (41–50 cm) chain, 2–4 mm links
- **2** 4–5 mm jump rings
- lobster claw clasp and soldered jump ring
- chainnose and roundnose pliers
- diagonal wire cutters
- Right Angle mandrel (Fiskars, fiskarscrafts.com) or round pen

Design alternative

Loop the ends of the 16-gauge wire in opposite directions before pulling the ends together. Hammer the wire for texture and string a chain through one loop.

Leafy
greens

A spring necklace grows from a simple component

by Lauren M. Hadley

I don't plan my designs. Instead, I find inspiration in my materials — in texture, contour, color, and shape. For this necklace, the brass leaf component was the starting point. I punched holes in the leaves to make a connector, and then I paired it with Russian amazonite beads for a beautiful color contrast.

1 necklace • On a decorative head pin, string a spacer, an oval bead, and a spacer. Make the first half of a wrapped loop (Basics, p. 12).

2 Attach the loop and the center loop of a leaf component. Complete the wraps.

3 Cut a 1-in. (2.5 cm) piece of wire. Make a plain loop (Basics) on one end. String a coin-shaped bead and make a plain loop perpendicular to the first loop. Make 10 coin units.

4 Cut ten ¾-in. (1.9 cm) pieces of chain. Open a jump ring (Basics). Attach a chain and a hole in the leaf. Close the jump ring. Repeat on the other side.

Supplies

necklace 20 in. (51 cm)
- 30 mm oval bead
- **10** 8 mm faceted coin-shaped beads
- **2** 4 mm flat spacers
- 10 in. (25 cm) 22- or 24-gauge half-hard wire
- 12–14 in. (30–36 cm) chain, 3 mm links
- 41 mm leaf component
- 2½-in. (6.4 cm) decorative head pin
- **4** 3–4 mm jump rings
- lobster claw clasp
- chainnose and roundnose pliers
- diagonal wire cutters

earrings
- **2** 8 mm faceted coin-shaped beads
- **4** 4 mm flat spacers
- **2** 1½-in. (3.8 cm) decorative head pins
- pair of earring wires
- chainnose and roundnose pliers
- diagonal wire cutters

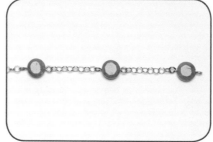

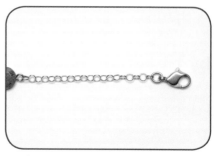

5 Open the loops of a coin unit. On each side, attach a chain and close the loop. On each side, attach the remaining coin units and chains.

6 Cut two 2–3-in. (5–7.6 cm) pieces of chain. On each end, attach a chain. Check the fit, and trim chain if necessary. On one end, use a jump ring to attach a lobster claw clasp. On the other end, attach a jump ring.

1 earrings • On a decorative head pin, string a coin-shaped bead and two spacers. Make a wrapped loop (Basics, p. 12).

2 Open the loop of an earring wire (Basics). Attach the dangle and close the loop. Make a second earring to match the first.

Tip

If you prefer autumnal shades, use gemstones in reds or browns. Poppy jasper, carnelian, or Botswana agate offer pretty color combinations.

66 Don't second-guess your creativity. Go with what you feel and let it flow rather than following what you think might sell. **99**

Become a
wrapped-loop
expert

Create a chain
with tiny loops and gemstones

by Salena Safranski

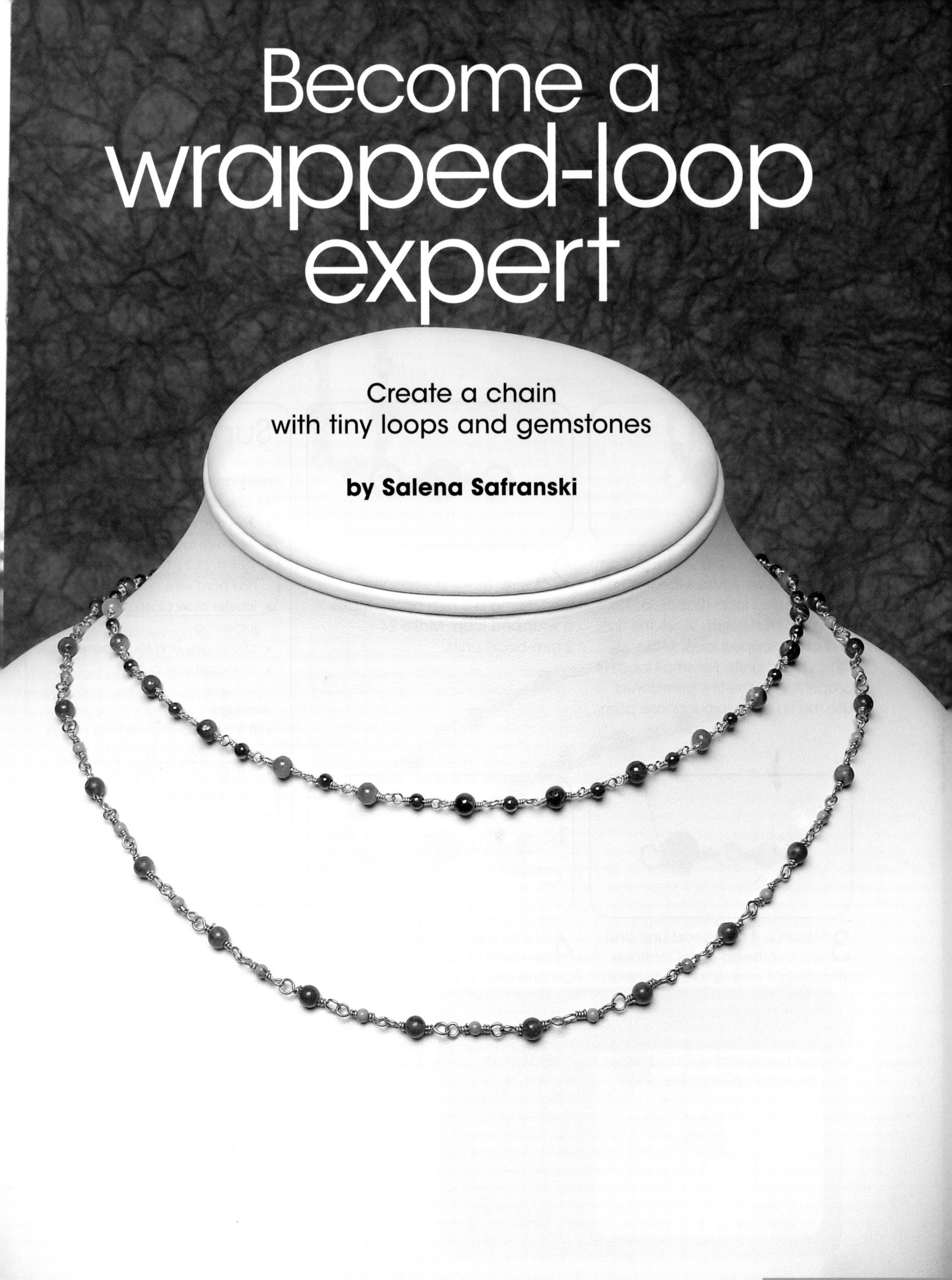

WIRE WORKS
like a charm

Draw fun little components in wire

by Laura Crook Woodard

Supplies

heart charm
- 5 in. (13 cm) 18-gauge half-hard wire
- craft wire to practice
- 6–7 mm jump ring
- chainnose, roundnose, and nylon-jaw pliers
- diagonal wire cutters

fish charm
- 7 in. (18 cm) 18-gauge half-hard wire
- craft wire to practice
- 6–7 mm jump ring
- chainnose, roundnose, and nylon-jaw pliers
- diagonal wire cutters

Anything you can draw on paper you can make with wire. All you need are pliers, wire, and lots of patience. Practice the two spiral techniques on page 131 with inexpensive craft wire, then make several prototypes of these heart and fish charms before making "the real deal" with sterling, gold-filled, or colored wire. The extra effort will build up your skills so they shine as brightly as your new charms!

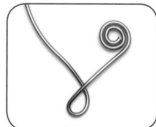

1 heart charm • Cut a 5-in. (13 cm) piece of wire and straighten it with nylon-jaw pliers. On one end, make an 8–10 mm tight spiral (p. 131). With your fingers, curve the wire as shown.

2 With roundnose pliers, grasp the wire ¾ in. (1.9 cm) below the spiral. Wrap the wire around the pliers to form a teardrop shape and curve the wire as shown.

3 On the end of the wire tail, make an 8–10 mm loose spiral (p. 131). Open a jump ring (Basics, p. 12), attach the charm, and close the jump ring.

   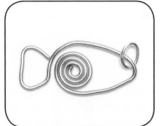

1 fish charm · Cut a 7-in. (18 cm) piece of wire and straighten it with nylon-jaw pliers. On one end, make a 10 mm tight spiral (below). With your fingers, curve the wire as shown.

2 With roundnose pliers, grasp the wire ¾ in. (1.9 cm) from the spiral and gently bend the wire as shown.

3 With chainnose pliers, grasp the wire and the spiral horizontally and curve the wire halfway around the spiral. Bend the wire away from the spiral as shown.

4 With chainnose pliers, bend the wire ¼ in. (6 mm) from the spiral as shown. Make a second bend ³⁄₈ in. (1 cm) from the first and trim the excess wire. Open a jump ring (Basics, p. 12), attach the charm, and close the jump ring.

Tight spiral

1. Grasp the end of the wire with the tip of your roundnose pliers. Rotate the pliers to form a loop. If the start of the loop is straight rather than rounded, trim it off and rotate the wire again.

2. Grasp the loop horizontally with chainnose pliers so that just the edge of the loop is visible. Press the next ⅛ in. (3 mm) of the wire tail against the loop.

3. Reposition the pliers and press the next ⅛ in. (3 mm) of the wire tail against the loop. Repeat until the spiral is the desired size.

Loose spiral

1. Repeat step 1 of "Tight spiral."
2. Repeat steps 2 and 3 of "Tight spiral," but do not press the wire tail

against the loop. Instead, leave a 1–2 mm gap between the loop and the wire tail.

Mix it up
Once you've mastered the tight and loose spiral, you can add wire wraps and beads to your designs, as in these snail and treble clef charms.

Three-ring
earrings

Jump rings and seed beads come together in chic earrings

by Amy Thompson

A favorite accessory doesn't have to be excessive in detail or cost. I love these earrings because they're inexpensive, they take no time at all to make, and they go with everything! Use two sizes of jump rings and some spare seed beads to make earrings of your chosen length (mine are just under 2 in./5 cm long). Simply add or remove jump rings for longer or shorter dangles.

1 Open a large jump ring (Basics, p. 12). String an 8º seed bead, three small jump rings, and an 8º. Close the jump ring.

2 Open another large jump ring and attach the three small jump rings from the first step. String 8ºs and small jump rings as in step 1, and close the large jump ring.

3 Repeat step 2 to add another large jump ring component. Continue adding jump ring components until the dangle is the desired length.

4 Open the loop of an earring wire (Basics) and attach the dangle. Close the loop. Make a second earring to match the first.

Supplies

- **6** 10–12 mm (large) jump rings
- **18** 5 mm (small) jump rings
- **12** 8º seed beads
- pair of earring wires
- chainnose and roundnose pliers, or **2** pairs of chainnose pliers

Tip

Make a matching bracelet by following steps 1 through 3. Use a small jump ring to attach a lobster claw clasp to one end.

Quick mix and

Coordinating necklaces look great together or separately

by Rupa Balachandar

Layered necklaces are a great look whether you're dressing up or down. These simple strands make a great mix-and-match team.

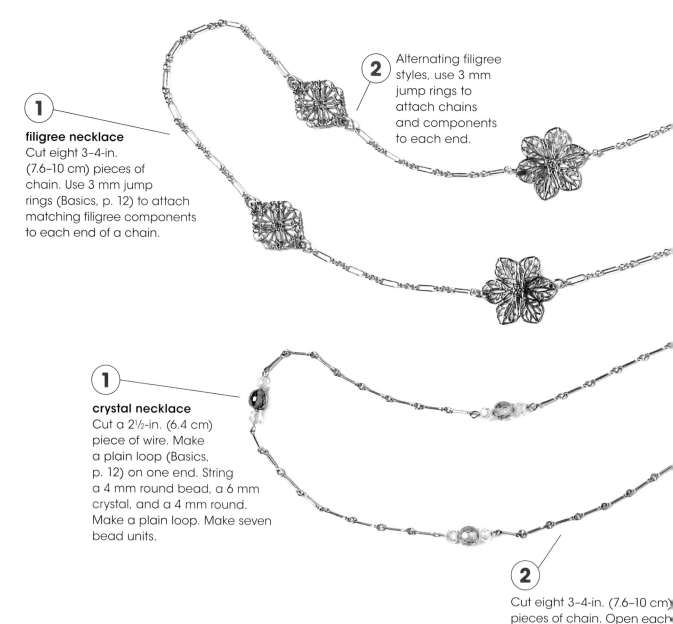

①

filigree necklace
Cut eight 3–4-in. (7.6–10 cm) pieces of chain. Use 3 mm jump rings (Basics, p. 12) to attach matching filigree components to each end of a chain.

②
Alternating filigree styles, use 3 mm jump rings to attach chains and components to each end.

①

crystal necklace
Cut a 2½-in. (6.4 cm) piece of wire. Make a plain loop (Basics, p. 12) on one end. String a 4 mm round bead, a 6 mm crystal, and a 4 mm round. Make a plain loop. Make seven bead units.

②
Cut eight 3–4-in. (7.6–10 cm) pieces of chain. Open each loop (Basics) of a bead unit and attach a chain. Close the loops.

match

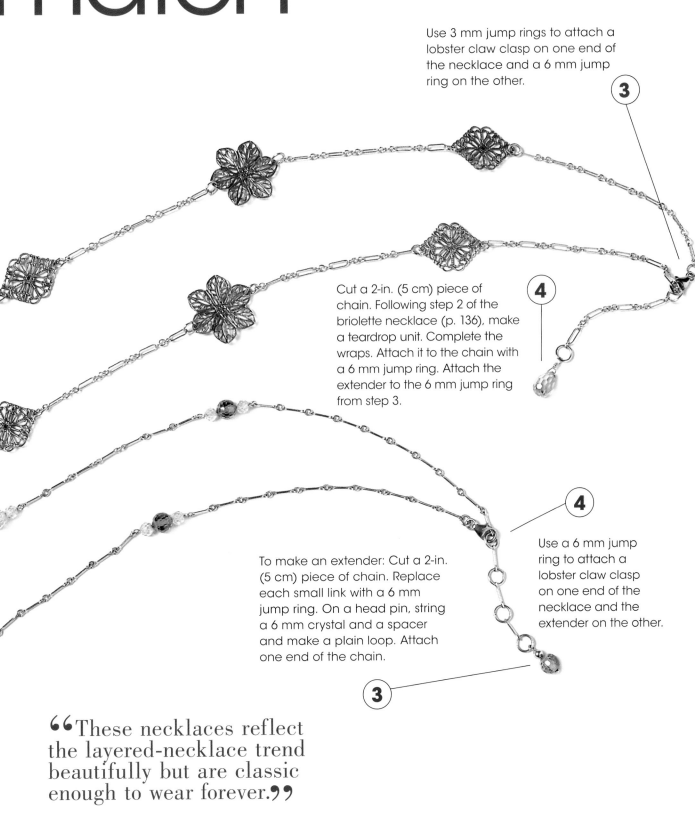

Use 3 mm jump rings to attach a lobster claw clasp on one end of the necklace and a 6 mm jump ring on the other.

3

Cut a 2-in. (5 cm) piece of chain. Following step 2 of the briolette necklace (p. 136), make a teardrop unit. Complete the wraps. Attach it to the chain with a 6 mm jump ring. Attach the extender to the 6 mm jump ring from step 3.

4

4

To make an extender: Cut a 2-in. (5 cm) piece of chain. Replace each small link with a 6 mm jump ring. On a head pin, string a 6 mm crystal and a spacer and make a plain loop. Attach one end of the chain.

Use a 6 mm jump ring to attach a lobster claw clasp on one end of the necklace and the extender on the other.

3

66These necklaces reflect the layered-necklace trend beautifully but are classic enough to wear forever.99

briolette necklace

On a head pin, string a spacer. Make the first half of a wrapped loop (Basics, p. 12). Make five spacer units.

Cut a 2½-in. (6.4 cm) piece of wire. String a briolette. Make a set of wraps above the bead (Basics). Make the first half of a wrapped loop. Make three briolette units in one color and two in a second color.

To make an extender: Cut a 1½-in. (3.8 cm) piece of chain. Attach a spacer unit to an end link and complete the wraps.

Cut a 15–17-in. (38–43 cm) piece of chain. Attach a briolette unit to the center link. Complete the wraps. On each side, attach spacer units and briolette units as shown, completing the wraps as you go.

Open a jump ring (Basics). On one end of the necklace, attach a lobster claw clasp and an end link of the chain. Close the jump ring. Repeat on the other end, substituting the extender for the clasp.

Arrange the components on a flat surface before attaching them.

earrings

Cut a 1-in. (2.5 cm) piece of wire. Make a plain loop (Basics, p. 12) on one end. String a spacer, a crystal, and a spacer. Make a plain loop.

Open a loop of the crystal unit (Basics) and attach a filigree component. Close the loop. Attach a different component to the remaining loop.

Open the loop of an earring wire. Attach the dangle and close the loop. Make a second earring to match the first.

Supplies

filigree necklace 38 in. (97 cm)
- 7–9 mm teardrop bead
- **10** 20–25 mm filigree components, in two styles
- 2½ in. (6.4 cm) 26-gauge half-hard wire
- 26–34 in. (66–86 cm) long-and-short-link chain
- **2** 6 mm jump rings
- **21** 3–4 mm jump rings
- lobster claw clasp
- chainnose and roundnose pliers
- diagonal wire cutters

crystal necklace 38 in. (97 cm)
- **8** 6 mm round crystals
- **14** 4 mm round crystals or gemstones
- 4 mm spacer
- 17½ in. (44.5 cm) 24-gauge half-hard wire
- 26–34 in. (66–86 cm) bar-and-link chain
- 1½-in. (3.8 cm) head pin
- **4** 6 mm jump rings
- lobster claw clasp
- chainnose and roundnose pliers
- diagonal wire cutters

briolette necklace 15½ in. (39.4 cm)
- **5** 7–9 mm briolettes
- **5** 4 mm stardust spacers
- 13 in. (33 cm) 26-gauge half-hard wire
- 17–19 in. (43–48 cm) fancy chain
- **5** 1½-in. (3.8 cm) head pins
- **2** 6 mm jump rings
- lobster claw clasp
- chainnose and roundnose pliers
- diagonal wire cutters

earrings
- **2** 6 mm round crystals
- **4** 3 mm spacers
- **4** 20–25 mm filigree components, in two styles
- 2 in. (5 cm) 24-gauge half-hard wire
- pair of earring wires
- chainnose and roundnose pliers
- diagonal wire cutters

Supplies for the gold necklaces from Rupa B. Designs, rupab.com. Silver chain and spacers from Amidhara Gems and Minerals, amidhara.com. Silver components from Nina Designs, ninadesigns.com.

Tip

The rose components in the silver necklace are actually charms. I removed the manufacturer's jump rings before I attached them to my chain segments.

> **"Instead of alternating components, try using different types of chain in the filigree necklace."**

Lovely links
Use different colors and styles of chain, links, and beads to make necklaces that match any outfit.

Mixed

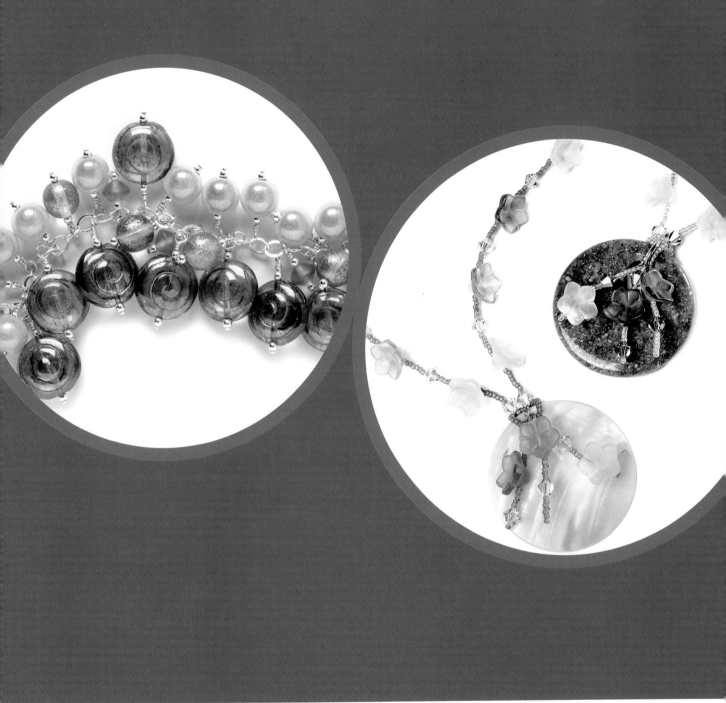

media

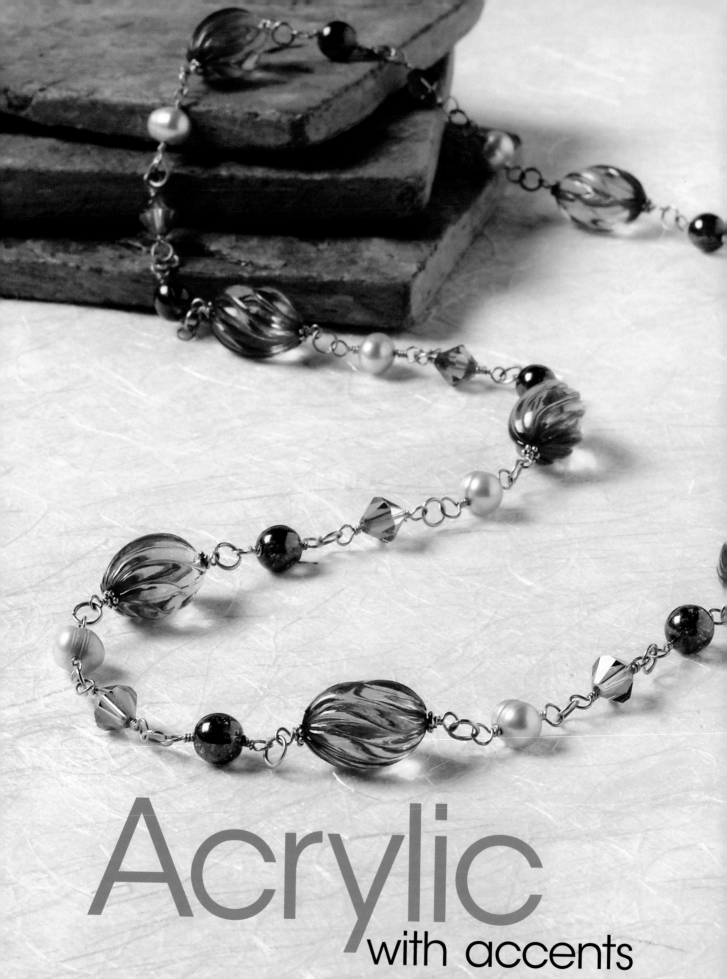

Acrylic
with accents

Make an affordable necklace with a few big, bubbly beads

by Jennifer Ortiz

Incorporating acrylic beads into a necklace is an inexpensive and lightweight design option. These large fluted-oval beads come in several colors. I used amber-colored beads in the necklace on this page and rust in the necklace at the left. Both are appropriate for an autumn palette. For a summery look, wear the shorter version with retro-pink acrylic beads.

1 necklace • Cut a 2½-in. (6.4 cm) piece of wire. Make a wrapped loop (Basics, p. 12) on one end. String a spacer, an oval bead, and a spacer. Make a wrapped loop. Make eight to 10 oval-bead units.

2 Cut a 2-in. (5 cm) piece of wire. Make a wrapped loop on one end. String a round bead. Make a wrapped loop. Repeat with a bicone crystal and a pearl. Make eight to 10 of each type of bead unit.

3 Open a jump ring (Basics). Attach an oval-bead unit and a round-bead unit. Close the jump ring. Use jump rings to attach a bicone unit, then a pearl unit. Repeat until the necklace is the desired length, then use a jump ring to attach the first and last bead units.

Tip

Silver wire is beautiful, but it can be expensive. To keep costs down, try using craft wire.

Supplies

**necklace (amber 13½ in./
34.3 cm; rust 18 in./46 cm)**
- ◆ **8–10** 20 mm acrylic oval beads
- ◆ **8–10** 8 mm bicone crystals
- ◆ **8–10** 8 mm potato pearls
- ◆ **8–10** 8 mm round beads
- ◆ **16–20** 4 mm flat spacers
- ◆ **68–85** in. (1.7–2.2 m) 24-gauge half-hard wire
- ◆ **32–40** 4 mm jump rings
- ◆ chainnose and roundnose pliers
- ◆ diagonal wire cutters

earrings
- ◆ **2** 8 mm bicone crystals
- ◆ **2** 8 mm potato pearls
- ◆ **2** 8 mm round beads
- ◆ **8** in. (20 cm) 24-gauge half-hard wire
- ◆ **2** 1½-in. (3.8 cm) head pins
- ◆ **4** 4 mm jump rings
- ◆ pair of lever-back earring wires
- ◆ chainnose and roundnose pliers
- ◆ diagonal wire cutters

1 earrings · On a head pin, string a pearl. Make a wrapped loop (Basics, p. 12).

Cut a 2-in. (5 cm) piece of wire. Make a wrapped loop on one end. String a bicone crystal. Make a wrapped loop. Repeat with a round bead.

2 Open a jump ring (Basics). Attach the pearl unit and the bicone unit. Close the jump ring.

3 Use a jump ring to attach the bicone unit and the round-bead unit.

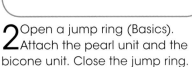

4 Open the loop of an earring wire (Basics). Attach the dangle and close the loop. Make a second earring to match the first.

Design alternative

Save time with this immediate-gratification version. String the same type of beads without all of the wrapped loops.

Branch out
for fall

A favorite story
inspires an autumn
necklace

by Melissa Lee

Bountiful
bracelet

Harvest pearls and crystals in autumn hues

by Katherine Schwartzenberger

Collect a bouquet of fall leaves, and they'll quickly fade. But make this bracelet-and-earrings set, and you'll enjoy the colors all season long. Silver tubes and spacers set off fiery fall colors. The spacers remind me of the beauty of the bare trees just around the corner, and curved-tube beads give the bracelet a natural arc. The stringing is simple, but be prepared to flex your wrapped-loop skills!

1 bracelet • On a 26-gauge head pin, string a pearl. Make a wrapped loop (Basics, p. 12). Make 18 pearl units. On a 26-gauge head pin, string a bicone crystal and a pearl. Make a wrapped loop. Make 12 bicone-and-pearl units.

2 On a 24-gauge head pin, string a bicone. Starting 3/16 in. (5 mm) above the bicone, make a wrapped loop. Make 11 bicone units. Repeat with a 4 mm (small) flat spacer to make six spacer units.

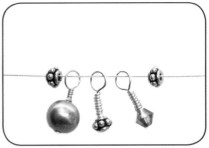

3 Cut a piece of beading wire (Basics). Center a small flat spacer, three wrapped-loop units, and a small flat spacer.

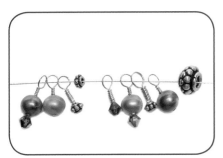

4 On each end, string three wrapped-loop units and a small flat spacer. Repeat five times. On each end, string four wrapped-loop units and a 6–9 mm (large) flat spacer.

5 On each end, string a tube bead. If your tube bead has a large diameter, string enough seed beads to fill the tube so the wire does not move as much inside.

6 On one end, string: large flat spacer, 5 mm round spacer, 3 mm round spacer, crimp bead, 3 mm round spacer, lobster claw clasp. Repeat on the other end, substituting a 1-in. (2.5 cm) piece of chain for the clasp. Check the fit, and add or remove beads if necessary. Go back through the last few beads strung and tighten the wire. Crimp the crimp beads (Basics) and trim the excess wire.

❝My sister was my inspiration. I wanted her to have a bracelet functional for desk work but still with a lot of detail.❞

Design alternative

The icy shades of turquoise jasper make this project the perfect winter gift. Plus, a single strand offers a range of hues, cutting down on costs.

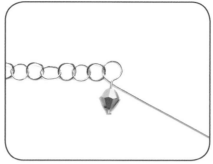

7 On a 24-gauge head pin, string a bicone. Make the first half of a wrapped loop. Attach the end link of the chain and complete the wraps.

Supplies

bracelet

- ◆ **30** 6 mm pearls, in two colors
- ◆ **24** 4 mm bicone crystals
- ◆ **4** 6–9 mm flat spacers
- ◆ **18** 4 mm flat spacers
- ◆ **2** 5 mm round spacers
- ◆ **4** 3 mm round spacers
- ◆ **2** 35–45 mm silver curved-tube beads
- ◆ 8º or 10º seed beads, to fill curved-tube beads (optional)
- ◆ flexible beading wire, .018 or .019
- ◆ 1 in. (2.5 cm) chain
- ◆ **19** 2-in. (5 cm) 24-gauge head pins
- ◆ **30** 2-in. (5 cm) 26-gauge head pins
- ◆ **2** crimp beads
- ◆ lobster claw clasp
- ◆ chainnose and roundnose pliers
- ◆ diagonal wire cutters
- ◆ crimping pliers (optional)

earrings

- ◆ **4** 6 mm pearls, in two colors
- ◆ **2** 4 mm bicone crystals
- ◆ **2** 4 mm flat spacers
- ◆ **2** 24-gauge head pins
- ◆ **2** 26-gauge head pins
- ◆ **2** 5 mm jump rings
- ◆ pair of earring wires
- ◆ chainnose and roundnose pliers
- ◆ diagonal wire cutters

1 earrings • On a 26-gauge head pin, string a bicone crystal and two pearls. Make a wrapped loop (Basics, p. 12). On a 24-gauge head pin, string a spacer. Starting ³/₁₆ in. (5 mm) above the spacer, make a wrapped loop.

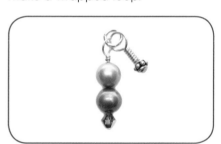

2 Open a jump ring (Basics) and attach the two wrapped-loop units. Close the jump ring.

3 Open the loop of an earring wire (Basics) and attach the dangle. Make a second earring to match the first.

Beaded beads
from Bali

An ancient craft fits
contemporary design perfectly

by Jane Konkel

Artisans from Bali make each of these beaded beads by weaving thousands of tiny glass seed beads around a plastic or wooden mold. Each bead takes up to three hours to make. Felt balls, made in Nepal, are a quiet contrast to the ornate beaded beads, while silver wire swirls and brushed rondelles unite the asymmetrical pattern.

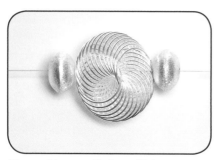

1 necklace • Cut an 18-in. (46 cm) piece of beading wire. String a 16 mm rondelle, a 36 mm wire spiral, and a rondelle.

2 On one end, string 7½ in. (19.1 cm) of beads.

3 On the other end, string 3 in. (7.6 cm) of beads.
Decide how long you want your necklace to be, subtract 12 in. (30 cm), and cut a piece of chain to that length. Cut the chain in half.

4 On each end of the beaded strand, string: spacer, crimp bead, spacer, Wire Guardian, chain. Go back through the last few beads strung and tighten the wire. Crimp the crimp bead (Basics, p. 12) and trim the excess wire. If desired, close a crimp cover over each crimp.

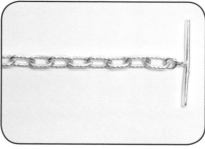

5 Check the fit, and trim chain from each end if necessary. On each end, open a jump ring (Basics) and attach the chain and half of a clasp. Close the jump ring.

Can you believe...
Larger beaded beads can take up to eight hours to weave.

"It's easy to appreciate the intricate designs of these beaded beads. Each one demonstrates the discipline and artistry of the craftspeople who make them."

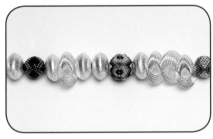

1 bracelet • Cut a piece of beading wire (Basics, p. 12). String 5–6½ in. (13–16.5 cm) of beads, allowing 1½ in. (3.8 cm) for finishing.

2 On each end, string: spacer, crimp bead, spacer, Wire Guardian, half of a clasp. Check the fit, and add or remove beads if necessary. Go back through the last few beads strung and tighten the wire. Crimp the crimp bead (Basics) and trim the excess wire. If desired, close a crimp cover over each crimp.

Design alternatives

Rubber tubing and a swivel clasp are less costly and formal than the chain and toggle clasp in the original necklace version.

Beaded beads with gold patterns look elegant strung on memory wire with gold tubes and cones.

Tips

• Use a tapestry needle to pierce a hole through the felt beads.
• Keep your necklace asymmetrical yet balanced. String the larger beads toward the center, and smaller beads on the ends of the beaded strand.

Supplies

necklace 25½ in. (64.8 cm)
◆ 36 mm wire spiral
◆ **2** 24 mm beaded beads
◆ **2** 20 mm beaded beads
◆ **4** 20 mm felt balls
◆ **2** 20 mm wire spirals
◆ **9** 16 mm rondelles
◆ 16 mm beaded bead
◆ **4** 3 mm round spacers
◆ flexible beading wire, .014 or .015
◆ 10–14 in. (25–36 cm) chain, 10–12 mm links
◆ **2** 5–6 mm jump rings
◆ **2** crimp beads
◆ **2** Wire Guardians
◆ toggle clasp
◆ chainnose or crimping pliers
◆ roundnose pliers
◆ diagonal wire cutters
◆ **2** crimp covers (optional)

bracelet
◆ **4** 20 mm wire spirals
◆ **6–10** 16 mm rondelles
◆ **3–4** 14–16 mm beaded beads
◆ **4** 3 mm round spacers
◆ flexible beading wire, .014 or .015
◆ **2** crimp beads
◆ **2** Wire Guardians
◆ toggle clasp
◆ chainnose or crimping pliers
◆ diagonal wire cutters
◆ **2** crimp covers (optional)

Beaded beads, felt balls, and toggle clasps shown from The Bead Goes On, beadgoeson.com. Silver-colored beads from Rings & Things, rings-things.com.

“These pieces were inspired by a spring wedding.**”**

Lucite flowers make a bright focal point.

Play up the beauty of a single blossom in a fresh necklace and earrings

by Lori Anderson

Pretty in pink

152

A Lucite flower forms the centerpiece of this lightweight necklace. Matte flowers are available in shades like tangerine, watermelon, and raspberry blush, offering you many options to accent a floral dress or make bridesmaid's jewelry. To complete the set without being too matchy-matchy, make earrings with a different kind of flower in a smaller size, but in the same shade.

1 necklace • On a decorative head pin, string a pearl. Make a wrapped loop (Basics, p. 12). Make five or six pearl units.

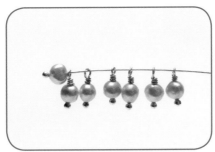

2 On a decorative head pin, string a pearl and the pearl units.

3 String a flower and a pearl. Make a wrapped loop. Bend the loop upward.

4 Decide how long you want your necklace to be and cut a piece of chain to that length. Open a jump ring (Basics). About 1 in. (2.5 cm) from the chain's center, attach a link and the loop of the pendant. Close the jump ring.

Supplies

necklace 16–18 in. (41–46 cm)
- 35–40 mm Lucite flower, center drilled
- **8-9** 4–5 mm round pearls
- 15–18 in. (38–46 cm) cable chain, 3–5 mm links
- **7-8** 1½-in. (3.8 cm) decorative head pins
- **2** 3–4 mm jump rings
- lobster claw clasp
- chainnose and roundnose pliers
- diagonal wire cutters

earrings
- **2** 15–25 mm Lucite flowers, center drilled
- **2** 4–5 mm round pearls
- **2** 1½-in. (3.8 cm) decorative head pins
- pair of earring wires
- chainnose and roundnose pliers
- diagonal wire cutters

Lucite flowers from The Beadin' Path, beadinpath.com.

or plum

5 Use a jump ring to attach the shorter end of the chain and a lobster claw clasp.

6 On a decorative head pin, string a pearl. Make the first half of a wrapped loop. Attach the dangle to the other end of chain and complete the wraps.

Tip

For a simpler pendant, skip the pearl units and string a crystal rondelle in the center.

1 earrings • On a decorative head pin, string a pearl and a flower. Bend the head pin upward.

Design alternative

Make earrings with Lucite petal beads on hoops. The color will appear darker as you layer additional petals.

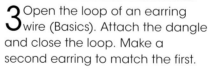

2 On the end of the head pin, make a wrapped loop (Basics, p. 12).

3 Open the loop of an earring wire (Basics). Attach the dangle and close the loop. Make a second earring to match the first.

Tip

The number of pearl units you'll need for the center of the flower will depend on the pearls' size — the larger they are, the fewer units you'll need to make.

Team a dragon pendant with exquisite capped beads

by **Jane Konkel**

labradorite

naga shell

crackle resin

copal

Repoussé riches from KATHMANDU

Nepal is among the poorest countries in the world. Nearly one-third of Nepalese people live in poverty. In 2006, Kate's Treasure started a partnership with a family of artisans living in Nepal, and has since extended the opportunity to other Tibetan and Nepalese families. These artisans practice the ancient art of repoussé — decorating metal by raising intricate shapes from the back with hammers and punches and adding details to the front by chasing or engraving. Because these exotic beads and beautiful pendants are handmade, each is slightly different.

1 necklace • Cut a piece of beading wire (Basics, p. 12). Center a tassel on the wire. Over both ends, string a 12 mm bead and a pendant.

2 On each end, string: 6 mm bead, 12 mm, 20 mm rondelle, 6 mm, 24 mm bead.

3 On each end, string: 22 mm bead, 36 mm bead, 6 mm, 18 mm bead, 12 mm.

4 On each end, string 6 mm beads until the strand is within 2 in. (5 cm) of the finished length.

5 On each end, string a crimp bead, a Wire Guardian, and half of a clasp. Check the fit, and add or remove beads if necessary. Go back through the last few beads strung and tighten the wire.

6 On each end, crimp the crimp bead (Basics) and trim the excess wire. Close a crimp cover over each crimp.

Supplies

necklace 19 in. (48 cm)
- 35 mm repoussé pendant
- **2** 36 mm silver-capped bicone beads
- **2** 24 mm flat oval beads
- **2** 22 mm silver-capped round beads
- **2** 20 mm silver-capped rondelles
- **2** 18 mm silver-capped round beads
- **5** 12 mm silver-capped round beads, in two colors
- **24–32** 6 mm round beads
- chain tassel
- flexible beading wire, .014 or .015
- **2** crimp beads
- **2** crimp covers
- **2** Wire Guardians
- toggle clasp
- chainnose or crimping pliers
- diagonal wire cutters

dangle earrings
- **2** 23 mm silver-capped bicone beads
- **2** 4 mm round beads
- **2** 2-in. (5 cm) decorative head pins
- pair of earring wires
- chainnose and roundnose pliers
- diagonal wire cutters

hoop earrings
- **2** 12 mm silver-capped round beads
- **4** 4 mm round beads
- pair of 32 mm earring hoops
- chainnose pliers

Repoussé beads and pendant from Kate's Treasure, katestreasure.com.

1 dangle earrings • On a decorative head pin, string a 4 mm bead and a 23 mm bead. Make a wrapped loop (Basics, p. 12).

2 Open the loop of an earring wire (Basics) and attach the dangle. Close the loop. Make a second earring to match the first.

1 hoop earrings • On an earring hoop, string a 4 mm bead, a 12 mm bead, and a 4 mm.

2 About ¼ in. (6 mm) from the end of the hoop, make a right-angle bend. Make a second earring to match the first.

Design alternative

I combined turquoise beads, beeswax amber beads, and gemstone chips in this extra-long strand. It's 33 in. (84 cm) and can be wrapped four times when worn as a bracelet or twice for a necklace.

The divine dragon

In Tibetan and Chinese mythology, the dragon was revered as a celestial creature. Many natural phenomena were attributed to the dragon's mood: Thirsty dragons caused droughts, angry dragons brought typhoons and floods, and happy, satisfied dragons delivered rain.

Ocean breeze
necklace

String a set in nature's watery hues
by Lorelei Eurto

Real sea urchins are usually 2–4 in. (5–10 cm) in size.

A beautiful sea urchin bead was the initial inspiration for this necklace. Then, as I looked through my bead bins, I realized that I already had many other ocean elements to include: gemstones that look like pebbles from the beach, a strand of tiny shells, beads reminiscent of sea glass, and a pewter button with a seaweed pattern. I set a few matching beads aside for the earrings, then strung a mix of sizes, shapes, and textures for an eclectic necklace.

1 **necklace** • Cut a piece of beading wire (Basics, p. 12). Center a metal accent bead, a sea urchin bead, and a metal bead.

2 On each end, string beads and spacers as desired until the necklace is within 1 in. (2.5 cm) of the finished length. Check the fit, and add or remove beads if necessary.

3 On one end, string: three 11º seed beads, crimp bead, four 11ºs, button, four 11ºs. Go back through the crimp bead and three 11ºs. Tighten the wire.

4 On the other end, string an 11º, a crimp bead, and enough 11ºs to make a loop large enough to accommodate the button. Go back through the crimp bead and the 11º. Tighten the wire. On each end, crimp the crimp bead (Basics) and trim the excess wire.

Design alternative

For easy mixing and matching, try Chinese sea glass disks and nuggets in shades of mint and seafoam.

Supplies

necklace 17 in. (43 cm)
- ◆ 25–30 mm sea urchin bead (Heather Powers, humblebeads.com)
- ◆ 15 mm button with shank
- ◆ **10–25** 6–25 mm glass beads
- ◆ **5–10** 10–13 mm gemstone beads
- ◆ **5–10** 8 mm metal accent beads
- ◆ **5–10** 6–8 mm shells
- ◆ 2 g 11º seed beads
- ◆ **5–10** 3–4 mm spacers
- ◆ flexible beading wire, .014 or .015
- ◆ **2** crimp beads
- ◆ chainnose or crimping pliers
- ◆ diagonal wire cutters

earrings
- ◆ **2** 9–12 mm glass beads
- ◆ **2** 5–6 mm glass beads
- ◆ **4** 3–4 mm spacers
- ◆ **2** 1½-in. (3.8 cm) head pins
- ◆ pair of earring wires
- ◆ chainnose and roundnose pliers
- ◆ diagonal wire cutters

1 **earrings** • On a head pin, string a spacer, a 5–6 mm glass bead, a 9–12 mm glass bead, and a spacer. Make a plain loop (Basics, p. 12).

2 Open the loop of an earring wire (Basics). Attach the dangle and close the loop. Make a second earring to match the first.

Pair a large
clasp with this
glass ring.

Bottles **POP** with
possibility

Explore your eco-friendly side with beads
made from repurposed bottles and caps

by Jane Konkel

Cathy Collison is a jewelry designer and the owner of Glass Garden Beads in Northfield, Minn. The bottle cap beads in these projects were her brainchild. When Cathy's "Aha!" moment struck, she ran a press release in the local paper: "Bead Lady Needs Bottle Caps," which encouraged people to "drink for the cause." Many of the bottle caps that people drop off have memories attached to them, so making the hand-crafted beads is well worth the effort.

1 bracelet • Cut a piece of beading wire (Basics, p. 12). String a 4 mm spacer, a glass bead, a 4 mm spacer, and a bottle cap bead. Repeat until the strand is within 2½ in. (6.4 cm) of the finished length.

2 On each end, string a crimp bead, a 4 mm spacer, and seven to 10 2 mm spacers.

❝You can join this repurposing effort: Send your bottle caps to Glass Garden Beads, 413 Division Street, Northfield, MN, 55057. Bottoms up!❞

Supplies

bracelet
- ◆ **4–5** 22 mm bottle cap beads
- ◆ **5–6** 8–16 mm Chinese sea glass spine drop beads (The Beadin' Path, beadinpath.com)
- ◆ 25 mm found-glass ring
- ◆ **12–14** 4 mm flat spacers
- ◆ **20** 2 mm faceted spacers
- ◆ flexible beading wire, .014 or .015
- ◆ **2** crimp beads
- ◆ **2** crimp covers
- ◆ 18 mm lobster claw clasp
- ◆ chainnose or crimping pliers
- ◆ diagonal wire cutters

necklace 18 in. (46 cm)
- ◆ 58 mm found-glass pendant
- ◆ 34 mm bottle cap heart pendant
- ◆ **7** 6 mm flat large-hole spacers
- ◆ 18-in. (46 cm) ball chain necklace with clasp
- ◆ **4** 7 mm jump rings
- ◆ **2** 5 mm jump rings
- ◆ **2** pairs of chainnose pliers or chainnose and bentnose pliers

earrings
- ◆ **2** 34 mm bottle cap heart pendants
- ◆ **2** 5 mm flat spacers
- ◆ **2** 4 mm flat spacers
- ◆ **2** 7 mm jump rings
- ◆ **2** 5 mm jump rings
- ◆ pair of 47 mm arched ear wires
- ◆ **2** pairs of chainnose pliers or chainnose and bentnose pliers

Bottle cap beads, pendants, found glass, and ball chain necklace from Glass Garden Beads, glassgardenbeads.com.

Tip

You can extend the length of your bracelet by attaching extra bead units to each end. Make the loops large enough to accommodate your lobster claw clasp.

3 On one end, string a glass ring. Go back through the spacer and crimp bead. Repeat on the other end, substituting a lobster claw clasp for the glass ring.

4 Check the fit, and add or remove beads if necessary. Tighten the wire. Crimp the crimp beads (Basics) and trim the excess wire. Close a crimp cover over each crimp.

1 necklace • Open a 7 mm jump ring (Basics, p. 12). Attach a glass pendant and a 5 mm jump ring. Close the 7 mm jump ring. Attach another 7 mm jump ring to the 5 mm jump ring. Repeat to make a heart dangle.

2 On a ball chain string: two 6 mm spacers, a dangle, three spacers, a dangle, two spacers.

Cathy's latest obsession is recycling vases and bottles into glass rings and pendants. She calls them found glass.

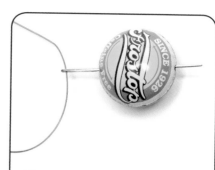

Tip

The bottle cap beads are hollow, so finding the hole when stringing them can be a challenge. Save time by using a sewing needle. The beading wire will kink, so start off with an extra 2–3 in. (5–7.6 cm) of wire.

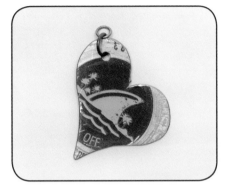

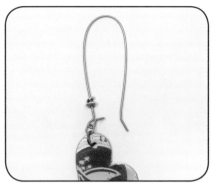

1 earrings • Open a 7 mm jump ring (Basics, p. 12). Attach a heart pendant and a 5 mm jump ring. Close the 7 mm jump ring.

2 String the heart dangle on an earring wire. Use chainnose pliers to gently close the loop of the earring wire.

3 String a 5 mm spacer and a 4 mm spacer on the earring wire. Make a second earring to match the first.

Design alternatives

A necklace for a bike-riding daughter.

A shark on a surfboard-shaped pendant for a swimming son.

A pair of earrings to wear when visiting Grandpa on Father's Day.

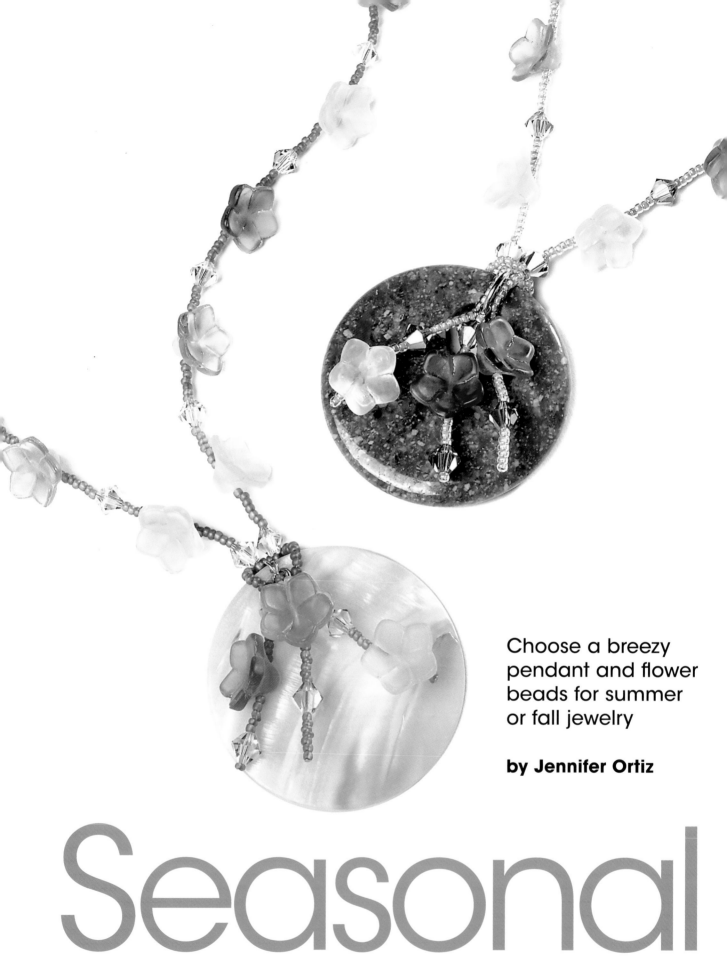

Choose a breezy
pendant and flower
beads for summer
or fall jewelry

by Jennifer Ortiz

Seasonal

Spend the last days of summer flaunting shells and suntans (safe, spray-on tans, of course). Show off both with a mother-of-pearl pendant decorated with pale flower beads. For a more earthy look, substitute a gemstone pendant for the shell.

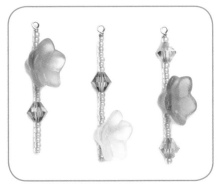

1 necklace • On a head pin, string: six 11º seed beads, bicone crystal, five 11ºs, flower bead, four 11ºs. Make a wrapped loop (Basics, p. 12). Make two more bead units as desired, staggering the colors and placement of the flowers.

2 Open a jump ring (Basics). Attach the bead units and a pendant and close the jump ring. If desired, curve the bead units slightly.

3 Decide how long you want your necklace to be. Add 8 in. (20 cm) and cut a piece of beading wire to that length. Center 1–2 in. (2.5–5 cm) of 11ºs. Over both ends, string the pendant. Pull the ends through the loop.

4 On each end, string a bicone, seven 11ºs, a flower bead, and seven 11ºs. Repeat, alternating flower colors, until the necklace is within 1 in. (2.5 cm) of the finished length. End with 11ºs.

5 On each end, string a crimp bead, an 11º, and half of a clasp. Check the fit, and add or remove beads from each end if necessary. Go back through the last few beads strung and tighten the wire. Crimp the crimp bead (Basics) and trim the excess wire.

> **"**I've done everything from oil painting to stained glass, enameling to crochet. I think I like beading best, especially at this point in my life, because it requires very little workspace.**"**

necklace

1 earrings • On a head pin, string: 11º seed bead, flower bead, seven 11ºs, bicone crystal, five 11ºs. Make a wrapped loop (Basics, p. 12).

2 Open the loop of an earring wire (Basics). Attach the dangle and close the loop. Make a second earring to match the first.

Tips

• Flower beads are available by the strand. Each strand has three colors, so it's easy to make a necklace in assorted shades.

• When you make the earring dangles, make enough wraps so that the beads stay in place and the flowers face forward.

Design alternative

Try vintage Lucite flowers strung with pearls for a delicate look.

Supplies

necklace (green pendant 17 in./43 cm; white pendant 18½ in./47 cm)

- 50 mm pendant, round or go-go style with large hole near the top
- **17–21** 15 mm flower beads (Jo-Ann Fabric and Craft Stores, joann.com for store locations)
- **18–22** 6 mm bicone crystals
- 2–3 g 11º seed beads
- flexible beading wire, .014 or .015
- **3** 2½-in. (6.4 cm) head pins
- 10–12 mm jump ring
- **2** crimp beads
- toggle clasp
- chainnose and roundnose pliers
- diagonal wire cutters
- crimping pliers (optional)

earrings

- **2** 15 mm flower beads (Jo-Ann Fabric and Craft Stores)
- **2** 6 mm bicone crystals
- 1 g 11º seed beads
- **2** 2½-in. (6.4 cm) head pins
- pair of lever-back earring wires
- chainnose and roundnose pliers
- diagonal wire cutters

Fiesta
necklace

Spin a festive 12-strand for
your next shindig

**by Rebecca
Conrad-LaMere**

Be ready to rumba when the next party comes around. Gather a gemstone go-go pendant and a hank of multicolored seed beads, then intersperse pops of navy, turquoise, and red. Your colorful necklace will have you looking salsa-smart in no time.

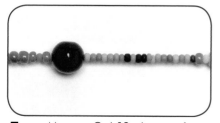

1 necklace • Cut 12 pieces of beading wire (Basics, p. 12). On one wire, string 11º seed beads, interspersing 8º seed beads and 9 mm round beads, until the strand is within 3 in. (7.6 cm) of the finished length.

2 On each of three wires, string 11ºs, interspersing 8ºs and 7 mm rounds, until each strand is within 3 in. (7.6 cm) of the finished length.

3 On each of six wires, string 11ºs, interspersing 8ºs and 5 mm rounds, until each strand is within 3 in. (7.6 cm) of the finished length.

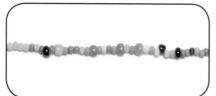

4 On each of two wires, string 11ºs, interspersing 8ºs, until each strand is within 3 in. (7.6 cm) of the finished length.
   Center a go-go pendant over all 12 strands.

5 Cut a 3-in. (7.6 cm) piece of 22-gauge wire. On one end, make a wrapped loop (Basics). On one side of each beaded strand, string a crimp bead, an 11º, and the loop. Repeat on the other side. Check the fit, and add or remove beads if necessary. Go back through the beads just strung and tighten the wires. Crimp the crimp beads (Basics) and trim the excess wire.

6 On one end, string a cone. Make a plain loop (Basics). Open a jump ring (Basics) and attach the loop and an S-hook clasp. Close the jump ring. Repeat on the other end, omitting the clasp.

1 earrings • Cut an 8-in. (20 cm) piece of beading wire. Center a round bead. On each end, string 1½ in. (3.8 cm) of 11º and 8º seed beads.

2 On each end, string a spacer. Over both ends, string a crimp bead and the loop of an earring wire. Go back through the crimp bead and tighten the wire.

3 Crimp the crimp bead (Basics, p. 12) and trim the excess wire. Close a crimp cover over the crimp. Make a second earring to match the first.

Supplies

necklace 20 in. (51 cm)
- 45–50 mm gemstone go-go pendant
- **4–8** 9 mm round beads
- **12–16** 7 mm round beads
- **32–38** 5 mm round beads
- 10 g 8º multicolored seed beads
- hank 11º multicolored seed beads, matte finish
- flexible beading wire, .014 or .015
- 6 in. (15 cm) 22-gauge half-hard wire
- **2** 6 mm jump rings
- **2** cones
- **24** crimp beads
- S-hook clasp
- chainnose and roundnose pliers
- diagonal wire cutters
- bead spinner (optional)
- crimping pliers (optional)

earrings
- **2** 9 mm round beads
- 2 g 8º multicolored seed beads
- 2 g 11º multicolored seed beads, matte finish
- **4** 4 mm spacers
- flexible beading wire, .014 or .015
- **2** crimp beads
- **2** crimp covers
- pair of earring wires
- chainnose or crimping pliers
- diagonal wire cutters

Design alternatives

Here are two earthy options: String three strands of 4–6 mm glass beads and 10 mm wood beads through an oval gold horn donut (shown on left side of this necklace). Or, loop four twisted strands of beads through the donut (shown on right side). Donut and wood beads from Rings & Things, rings-things.com. Orange beads from Happy Mango Beads, happymangobeads.com.

Tip

There are about 4,000 11º seed beads on a hank. If you enjoy designing with seed beads, consider using a time-saving bead spinner to string them onto your beading wire.

> **"This was my first project using my bead spinner, so I wanted to make a necklace with lots of seed beads."**

Tibetan prayer wheel pendant

A mixed-metal necklace makes a beautiful statement

by Rupa Balachandar

The prayer wheel is a Buddhist ritual instrument embossed with the Sanskrit words "Om mani padme hum," a prayer that invokes compassion. To receive the benefit of this prayer, the wheel must be set in motion. The inside of my pendant holds a prayer scroll for peace and protection. Each revolution of the wheel is considered to be as beneficial as speaking the mantra aloud.

1 necklace • On a head pin, string a 5 mm flat spacer, a pendant, and a flat spacer. Make a wrapped loop (Basics, p. 12). Cut a piece of beading wire (Basics) and center the pendant unit and a 3 mm spacer.

2 On each end, string: 4–5 mm fancy spacer, 3 mm spacer, bead cap, 3 mm spacer, 16 mm bead.

3 On each end, string a flat spacer, a fancy spacer, a flat spacer, and a 16 mm.

4 On each end, string a fancy spacer, an accent bead, a fancy spacer, and a 16 mm. Repeat step 3.

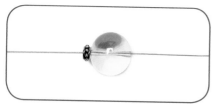

5 On each end, string a flat spacer and a 16 mm, repeating until the strand is within 2 in. (5 cm) of the finished length.

6 On each end, string: flat spacer, fancy spacer, flat spacer, crimp bead, flat spacer, crimp bead, half of a clasp. Check the fit, and add or remove beads if necessary. Go back through the last few beads strung and tighten the wire. Crimp the crimp beads (Basics) and trim the excess wire.

Supplies

necklace 19 in. (48 cm)
- 45 mm prayer wheel pendant
- **19** 16 mm round Lucite beads
- **2** 12 mm accent beads
- **26** 5 mm flat spacers
- **16** 4–5 mm fancy spacers
- **3** 3 mm round or nugget spacers
- **2** 6–8 mm bead caps
- flexible beading wire, .014 or .015
- 3-in. (7.6 cm) head pin
- **4** crimp beads
- toggle clasp
- **2** Wire Guardians (optional)
- chainnose and roundnose pliers
- diagonal wire cutters
- crimping pliers (optional)

earrings
- **2** 12 mm accent beads
- **2** 5 mm flat spacers
- **2** 4–5 mm fancy silver spacers
- **2** 2-in. (5 cm) head pins
- pair of earring wires
- chainnose and roundnose pliers
- diagonal wire cutters

Supplies from Rupa B. Designs, rupab.com.

1 earrings • On a head pin, string a 5 mm flat spacer, a 4–5 mm fancy spacer, and an accent bead. Make a wrapped loop (Basics, p. 12).

2 Open the loop of an earring wire (Basics). Attach the dangle and close the loop. Make a second earring to match the first.

Tips

• If you can't find a metal accent bead you like, consider stacking three or four fancy flat spacers.
• You may want to use two crimp beads on each side of the necklace for extra security because of the large pendant. Consider using Wire Guardians to add even more strength to your finishing.

"I enjoy designing jewelry that makes a statement, and this fabulous necklace will certainly garner some attention!"

Fair-weather trend

Combine bright beads
and textured
silver rings in a
summery necklace
and earrings

by Susan Kennedy

My handmade beads, with silver dots against a turquoise blue background, remind me of the ocean and grains of bright sand. I included a combination of shapes and textures: Hammered rings, twisted-wire jump rings, and disks and square beads exist harmoniously in one design. Repeat the brilliant color in a pair of simple drop earrings.

1a necklace • Cut a 4-in. (10 cm) piece of wire. Make a wrapped loop (Basics, p. 12). String a spacer, a disk bead, and a spacer. Make the first half of a wrapped loop. Make two units.

b Repeat step 1a, making a wrapped loop on each end. Make two units.

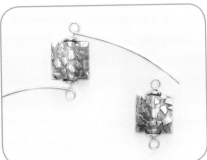

2a Cut a 3-in. (7.6 cm) piece of wire. Make the first half of a wrapped loop. String a square bead. Make the first half of a wrapped loop. Make four or six units.

b Repeat step 2a, making a wrapped loop on each end. Make two units.

3 Open a 7 mm jump ring (Basics). Attach a 1½-in. (3.8 cm) hammered ring and a twisted round jump ring. Close the jump ring. Repeat.

4 On each side, use a jump ring to attach the twisted round jump ring and a loop of a disk unit from step 1b. Using jump rings, attach: other loop of the disk unit, ¾-in. (1.9 cm) hammered ring, square-bead unit from step 2b, wrapped loop of a disk unit from step 1a.

5 On each side, attach a twisted oval jump ring, a square-bead unit from step 2a, a twisted round jump ring, and a square-bead unit from step 2a. Complete the wraps as you go. Repeat until the necklace is within 1½ in. (3.8 cm) of the finished length.

6 Check the fit, and add or remove square-bead units or jump rings if necessary. On one end, use a jump ring to attach a lobster claw clasp. Repeat on the other end, substituting a soldered jump ring for the clasp.

> **"**Go with a design you like, even if you think it's too different — you can always rework something after you get it down.**"**

1 earrings · On a head pin, string a spacer, a disk bead, and a spacer. Make a wrapped loop (Basics, p. 12).

2 Open the loop of an earring wire (Basics). Attach the dangle and close the loop. Make a second earring to match the first.

Supplies

necklace 16½ in. (41.9 cm)
- **4** 18 mm disk beads (Susan Kennedy, suebeads.com)
- **6–8** 11–12 mm square beads
- 1½-in. (3.8 cm) hammered ring
- **2** ¾-in. (1.9 cm) hammered rings
- **8** 3–4 mm round spacers
- 34–40 in. (.86–1 m) 24-gauge wire
- **4–6** 13 mm twisted round jump rings
- **4** 13 mm twisted oval jump rings
- **12** 7 mm jump rings
- lobster claw clasp and soldered jump ring
- chainnose and roundnose pliers
- diagonal wire cutters

earrings
- **2** 15 mm disk beads (Susan Kennedy)
- **4** 3–4 mm round spacers
- **2** 2-in. (5 cm) head pins
- pair of earring wires
- chainnose and roundnose pliers
- diagonal wire cutters

Design alternative

Handmade beads in shades of coral add a pop of color to a bracelet. Beads from suebeads.com.

Tip

For a decorative touch, use a textured jump ring in the necklace finish. You can make your own by hammering a soldered jump ring.

Chain jewelry features an assortment of colorful beads

by Lori Anderson

Clusters
& color

Fashionista
FRIDA

Flowers bloom
from crimson shell
pearls in homage
to a style icon

by Jane Konkel

ARTISTIC INSPIRATION

The paintings of Frida Kahlo tell the story of her psychological and physical turmoil, but her flamboyant fashion sense was a provocative contrast. Throughout her life, Frida identified with her Mexican heritage, dressing in native clothing like ankle-length tiered skirts, embroidered peasant blouses, and oversized beaded necklaces in bright colors reminiscent of her homeland. A band of mammoth blossoms was Frida's trademark tiara. Make a Frida-style statement piece with vintage Lucite flowers, blood-red beads, and enameled and patinated metals. Small-scale earrings extend the theme without being over-the-top.

1 necklace • For each of the black flower pendants, open a jump ring (Basics, p. 12), attach the pendant, and close the jump ring.

On a decorative head pin, string four or five center-drilled flowers. Make a wrapped loop (Basics). Make five to seven flower units.

2 Cut a piece of beading wire (Basics). Center an 8 mm round bead, the largest flower unit, and an 8 mm.

3 On each end, string an 8 mm, a flower unit, and an 8 mm. Repeat twice.

4 On each end, string an 8 mm and a 12 mm round bead. String 16 mm round beads until the strand is within 3 in. (7.6 cm) of the finished length.

5 On each end, string: 12 mm, crimp bead, 12 mm, Wire Guardian, half of a clasp. Check the fit, and add or remove beads from each end if necessary. Go back through the beads just strung and tighten the wire. Crimp the crimp bead (Basics) and trim the excess wire.

Tips

• Avoid making your necklace too long. In a short necklace, the flowers will hang flat at your collar and will be less likely to flip over.
• To design your own necklace, choose colors from your favorite artist's palette.

1 earrings • On a decorative head pin, string an 8 mm round bead, an 18 mm flower, and a 19 mm flower. Make a right-angle bend close to the flower.

2 Starting about 1¼ in. (3.2 cm) from the end of the head pin, make a wrapped loop (Basics, p. 12) parallel with the flower.

3 Open the loop of an earring wire (Basics) and attach the dangle. Close the loop. Make a second earring to match the first.

Design alternative

For this version, I wanted a tidier row of flowers rather than a bib-style necklace. So, instead of attaching jump rings to some of the pendants, I strung the wrapped loop of each flower unit. I also attached a dangle to the hole of each flower and strung a few more 8 mm beads between the flower units.

Flower arranging

- When stacking flowers, alternate metal with Lucite.
- For a lush look, stack five or more flowers.
- Layer flowers of different colors to create dimension.
- For a more conservative necklace, string flowers of approximately the same size, in a limited palette.
- For a simple variation, attach one layered-flower pendant from a chain.

Design alternative

I strung a strand of yellow button pearls and crystals through large-link plastic chain. Next, I attached the wrapped loop of a single lucite flower to the yellow strand for a necklace that's bold but less blooming.

Supplies

necklace 18 in. (46 cm)
- **3** 57–72 mm black metal flower pendants
- **5** 42–52 mm brass and copper flowers
- **8–10** 20–40 mm plastic, Lucite, or metal flowers
- **12–15** 10–19 mm plastic, Lucite, or metal flowers
- **10–14** 16 mm round shell pearls
- **6** 12 mm round shell pearls
- **19** 8 mm round shell pearls
- flexible beading wire, .018 or .019
- **7** 2-in. (5 cm) decorative head pins

- **3** 4 mm jump rings
- **2** crimp beads
- **2** Wire Guardians
- hook-and-eye clasp
- chainnose and roundnose pliers
- diagonal wire cutters
- crimping pliers (optional)

earrings
- **2** 19 mm plastic flowers
- **2** 18 mm plastic flowers
- **2** 8 mm round shell pearls

- **2** 2-in. (5 cm) decorative head pins
- pair of earring wires
- chainnose and roundnose pliers
- diagonal wire cutters

Lucite and metal flowers and pendants from The Beadin' Path, beadinpath.com

66Had I accessorized Frida Kahlo, I would have started with pieces similar to these.**99**

Put on a
happy
vase

A handful of beads and some elastic cord are all you need to create a quick accent

by Steven James

This super quick project is not only a great way to make a dent in your bead stash, but it's also a low-commitment opportunity for color and design experimentation. Play with harmonious and contrasting patterns. See how the impact changes when you combine different shapes, sizes, and textures. You can even layer vaselets for a more lush look.

1 Measure the neck of a vase and add 6 in. (15 cm). Cut a piece of elastic cord to that length.

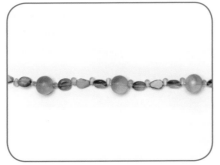

2 String enough beads to go all the way around the vase. Check the length, and add or remove beads if necessary.

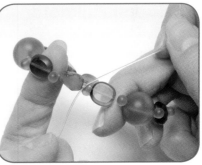

3 Tie a surgeon's knot (Basics, p. 12) and dot the knot with glue. Trim the excess elastic.

Tips

Make a vaselet when you:
- need a quick hostess gift
- want to color-coordinate centerpieces at your wedding
- need a favor or a fun activity at a baby shower
- want a contrast with the colors of a bouquet
- want to update a favorite vase for each season

Supplies

- beads in a variety of shapes and sizes
- elastic cord
- diagonal wire cutters or scissors
- G-S Hypo Cement
- tape measure

Heartwarming
HOLIDAY

Show your love with heart-themed ornaments

by Naomi Fujimoto

Decorating the tree is my favorite part of the holiday season. (Though, baking cookies runs a close second.) I'm a big fan of hearts, and I think the winter holidays are as good a time as Valentine's Day to show it. A vintage-looking key and a certain red-nosed reindeer also make great ornaments when paired with chain and charms.

1 glass-heart ornament • String a heart pendant on a hoop earring.

2 Cut a 9–11-in. (23–28 cm) piece of beading wire. String assorted beads as desired.

3 On each end, string a crimp bead and a spacer. Over both ends, string a soldered jump ring. Go back through the last few beads strung and tighten the wire. Crimp the crimp beads (Basics, p. 12) and trim the excess wire.

4 With chainnose pliers, close a crimp cover over each crimp. Open the hoop earring. Attach the jump ring and close the hoop.

1 key ornament • On a bench block or anvil, hammer each side of a heart link.

2 Cut a 3-in. (7.6 cm) piece of wire. Holding one end with chainnose pliers, wrap the other end around the heart a few times.

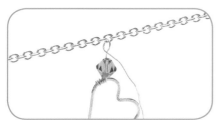

3 String a crystal and make the first half of a wrapped loop (Basics, p. 12). Cut an 8-in. (20 cm) piece of chain. About 1 in. (2.5 cm) from one end, attach the heart unit and complete the wraps.

4 Open a jump ring (Basics). Attach each end of the chain. Close the jump ring.

Use a jump ring to attach the first jump ring and a key pendant.

1 deer ornament • Following the manufacturer's instructions, use epoxy to glue a flatback crystal to the deer pendant. Open a jump ring (Basics, p. 12). Attach the pendant and close the jump ring.

2 Cut a 9-in. (23 cm) piece of chain. String a word bead. Use a jump ring to attach each end of the chain and the first jump ring.

3 Use a jump ring to attach a heart charm and the chain.

Design alternative

Turn a brooch into an ornament by stringing a brooch converter.

Supplies

glass-heart ornament
- 40–50 mm heart pendant
- **19–25** 6–10 mm beads
- **2** 3–4 mm round spacers
- flexible beading wire, .014 or .015
- 3–4 mm soldered jump ring
- **2** crimp beads
- **2** crimp covers
- 20 mm oval-shaped hoop earring
- chainnose or crimping pliers
- diagonal wire cutters

key ornament
- 60–70 mm key pendant
- 5 mm bicone crystal
- 15 mm heart link (Rings & Things, rings-things.com)
- 3 in. (7.6 cm) 26-gauge dead-soft wire
- 8 in. (20 cm) chain, 2–3 mm links
- **2** 4–5 mm jump rings
- chainnose and roundnose pliers
- diagonal wire cutters
- bench block or anvil
- hammer

deer ornament
- 50 mm deer pendant
- 24 mm word bead (Ornamentea, ornamentea.com)
- 10–15 mm heart charm
- 3 mm flatback crystal
- 9 in. (23 cm) chain, 2–3 mm links
- **2** 4–5 mm jump rings
- chainnose and roundnose pliers, or **2** pairs of chainnose pliers
- diagonal wire cutters
- two-part epoxy

Pendants from Jo-Ann Fabric and Craft Stores, joann.com.

Charm aplenty

Premade clusters work
like a charm

by Jennifer Ortiz

I was at a craft store looking for sewing supplies when I spotted this premade charm cluster. I think it was originally designed as a purse dangle, but it looks great on a necklace! One cluster will give a necklace all the charm it needs, but you can buy a pair to make instant earrings.

1 necklace • On a head pin, string a bicone crystal. Make the first half of a wrapped loop (Basics, p. 12). Make four bicone units and four helix units.

2 Decide how long you want your necklace to be and cut a piece of chain to that length. Open the center link of chain as you would a jump ring (Basics) and attach a charm cluster. Close the link.

Supplies

necklace 18 in. (46 cm)
- charm cluster on 22 mm ring
- **4** 8 mm bicone crystals
- **4** 8 mm helix crystals
- 16–19 in. (41–48 cm) chain, 7–9 mm links
- **8** 1½-in. (3.8 cm) head pins
- toggle clasp
- chainnose and roundnose pliers
- diagonal wire cutters

earrings
- **2** 8 mm bicone crystals
- **2** 8 mm helix crystals
- 5 in. (13 cm) chain, 7–9 mm links
- **4** 1½-in. (3.8 cm) head pins
- **2** 5–6 mm jump rings
- pair of earring wires
- chainnose and roundnose pliers
- diagonal wire cutters

3 On one side, attach a bicone unit to a link ¾ in. (1.9 cm) from the center. Complete the wraps. Repeat on the other side.

4 On each side, attach a helix unit, a bicone unit, and a helix unit, skipping a link between units.

5 Check the fit, and trim chain if necessary. On each end, open a link and attach half of a clasp. Close the link.

Tip

In step 4 of the necklace, you don't need to attach crystal units to the same side of the chain. Using opposite sides of the chain will lend the necklace a less conventional look.

"I like to build off of one interesting piece, and just go from there."

1 earrings • Follow step 1 of the necklace to make a bicone unit and a helix unit.

2 Cut a ¾-in. (1.9 cm) and a 1¼-in. (3.2 cm) piece of chain. Attach a crystal unit to one end of each chain and complete the wraps.

3 Open a jump ring (Basics, p. 15). Attach each chain and the loop of an earring wire. Close the jump ring. Make a second earring the mirror image of the first.

Design alternative

For super easy earrings, buy two matching charm clusters. Attach each to an earring wire and you're done — no loops to turn, no chain to measure.

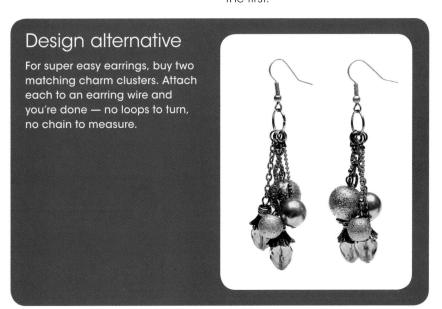

Bold bangle

Flaunt photos on your wrist with a chunky framed bracelet

by Jane Konkel

1 Punch or cut out an image to fit within a picture-frame link. Apply a thin coat of adhesive to the picture frame. Lay the image in the picture frame, pressing the image so that all of the edges lie flat. Allow the glue to dry.

2 Squeeze a little Diamond Glaze onto scrap paper to release any air bubbles. Slowly fill the picture frame with Diamond Glaze, completely covering the image all the way to the edges of the frame. Do not overfill the frame with glaze.

3 If bubbles appear in the glaze, use a toothpick to pop them before the glaze starts to set. Let the glaze set for 2–3 hours on a level surface. Make five picture frame links.

4 Open a 5 mm jump ring (Basics, p. 12) and attach the top loop of a frame and a loop of a 21 mm link. Close the jump ring. Use a second jump ring to attach the frame's top loop and another link. Repeat with the frame's bottom loop.

5 Use jump rings to attach the remaining frames and links.

Tips

• If you're printing a picture, use non-water-soluble inks. Images printed with an ink-jet printer will bleed. To prevent color bleed, you can also seal the image in clear packing tape first.

• Use a ½-in. (1.3 cm) paper punch to evenly punch out square images.

• Do not shake the Diamond Glaze. Bubbles will form.

• Try using different materials such as photos, stamps, or playing cards. Add crystals, beads, or charms for dimension.

Supplies

bracelet

- ◆ **5** 27 x 20 mm picture-frame links with two loops
- ◆ **12** 21 mm links with two loops
- ◆ **2** 19 x 17 mm triangular links with three loops
- ◆ 7 mm jump ring
- ◆ **25** 5 mm jump rings
- ◆ lobster claw clasp
- ◆ **2** pairs of pliers (may include chainnose, roundnose, and/or bentnose pliers)
- ◆ adhesive
- ◆ decorative paper or images
- ◆ Diamond Glaze
- ◆ square paper punch or scissors
- ◆ toothpick

Supplies from Fusion Beads, fusionbeads.com.

I used antique-copper-plated components, but rhodium-plated and gold-plated components are also available.

Adjusting the length

The materials listed here yield an 8-in. (20 cm) bracelet. You can shorten your bracelet by substituting jump rings for each triangular link, or by attaching four picture-frame links instead of five. Lengthen your bracelet by attaching additional jump rings to each end.

6 On one end, use jump rings to attach each link and two loops of a triangular link. Repeat on the other end.

7 On one end, use a jump ring to attach a lobster claw clasp. Attach a 7 mm jump ring on the other end.

66 Turn picture-frame links on their sides for a picture-perfect bracelet. 99

Delicate Drops

Make elegant chandelier earrings

by Naomi Fujimoto

1 earrings • Cut a 3-in. (7.6 cm) piece of wire. String a briolette and make a set of wraps above it (Basics, p. 12).

2 String a bicone crystal and make the first half of a wrapped loop (Basics) perpendicular to the briolette's holes.

3 Repeat steps 1 and 2 to make five briolette units.

4 Attach a briolette unit to the bottom center loop of a filigree component. Complete the wraps.

5 Attach the remaining briolette units to the remaining bottom loops of the filigree.

6 Open the loop of an earring wire (Basics). Attach the dangle and close the loop. Make a second earring to match the first.

I used cubic zirconia and dyed quartz briolettes in these lightweight earrings.

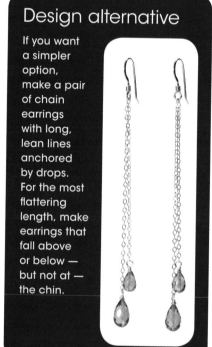

Design alternative

If you want a simpler option, make a pair of chain earrings with long, lean lines anchored by drops. For the most flattering length, make earrings that fall above or below — but not at — the chin.

Supplies

earrings
- **10** 9–12 mm briolettes
- **10** 3 mm bicone crystals
- 30 in. (76 cm) 26-gauge half-hard wire
- **2** 30–50 mm filigree components with five loops (Fire Mountain Gems and Beads, firemountain-gems.com.)
- pair of earring wires
- chainnose and roundnose pliers
- diagonal wire cutters

Tip

If you're using briolettes in different colors, make the second earring the mirror image of the first.

" Drop earrings are flattering because they elongate a round face. **"**

Button ring

Create fun and funky art for your fingers

by Cathy Jacicik

Tip

If the shell wiggles on the ring-base loop, add a drop of epoxy to keep it secure.

Supplies

button ring
- 3 25–40 mm flat buttons in different sizes
- ring base with disk
- two-part epoxy

shell ring
- 45 mm shell button
- 4–6 10 mm rondelles
- 6 in. (15 cm) 24-gauge half-hard wire
- ring base with loop
- roundnose pliers
- diagonal wire cutters

1 button ring • Using two-part epoxy, glue a stack of three buttons together. Let the epoxy dry.

2 Glue the disk of a ring base to the bottom of the button stack.

1 shell ring • Cut a 6-in. (15 cm) piece of wire. Center the loop of a ring base on the wire. Bring each end up through each hole of a shell button.

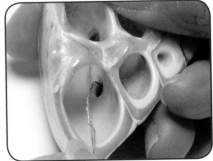

2 Twist the two wire ends together tightly to anchor the loop of the ring base above one hole of the shell.

> **"A bold ring can show your sense of humor as well as your sense of style."**

3 String rondelles over the twisted wire so that the last rondelle is visible above the shell.

4 Trim the wire tails to 1 in. (2.5 cm). Using roundnose pliers, coil the ends against the rondelle.

Wafer of options

Polymer clay beads pop on a simple chain

by Heather Powers

I love finding new ways to incorporate my handmade clay wafers into unique pieces of jewelry. The beads in this design capture the movement and colors of rolling ocean waves. Like the sea, much lies beneath this necklace's surface: seed beads, wire, and round beads. Buoyed by these components, the wafers seem to float on the neckline.

1 necklace • On a head pin, string a flat spacer and a wafer bead. Make a plain loop (Basics, p. 12). Make three wafer units.

2 Cut an 8-in. (20 cm) piece of 20- or 22-gauge wire. Center a wafer unit. On each end, string four or five 11º seed beads, a round bead, four or five 11ºs, and a wafer unit.

3a On one end, string eight to 10 11ºs and an accent bead. Make the first half of a wrapped loop (Basics).

b Cut two 7-in. (18 cm) pieces of chain. Attach one chain end and the loop. Complete the wraps.

4 On the other end, string five 11⁰s and a round. Make the first half of a wrapped loop. Attach a chain and complete the wraps.

5 Check the fit, and trim chain if necessary. Open a jump ring (Basics). Attach one chain end and a lobster claw clasp. Close the jump ring. Repeat on the other end, substituting a soldered jump ring for the clasp.

1 bracelet • Cut two pieces of chain. Follow necklace step 1 to make a wafer unit. Open the loop of the wafer unit (Basics, p. 12) and attach the center link of both chains.

2 Open a jump ring (Basics). On one end, attach both chains and a lobster claw clasp. Close the jump ring. Repeat on the other end, substituting a soldered jump ring for the clasp.

Supplies

necklace 19–21 in. (48–53 cm)
- **3** 1-in. (2.5 cm) wafer beads
- **6–10 mm** accent bead or button
- **3** 6 mm round beads
- **1 g** 11⁰ seed beads
- **3** 3 mm flat spacers
- **8 in. (20 cm)** 20- or 22-gauge half-hard wire
- **14–16 in. (36–41 cm)** chain, 2–3 mm links
- **3** 2-in. (5 cm) head pins
- **2** 3–4 mm jump rings
- lobster claw clasp and soldered jump ring
- chainnose and roundnose pliers
- diagonal wire cutters

bracelet
- **1-in. (2.5 cm)** wafer bead
- **3 mm** flat spacer
- **12–16 in. (30–41 cm)** chain, 2–3 mm links
- **2-in. (5 cm)** head pin
- **2** 4–5 mm jump rings
- lobster claw clasp and soldered jump ring
- chainnose and roundnose pliers
- diagonal wire cutters

Wafer beads from Humble Beads, humblebeads.com. Pewter button in silver necklace from Mamacita Beadworks, mamacitabeadworks. etsy.com.

Tip

Adjust the chain's length so the wire and wafer beads rest on your collarbone. Use a chain extender if you're making the necklace for someone else.

Design alternative

You can create earrings using similar wafer beads. Explore the other jewelry possibilities with this unique bead! (Earrings by Ann Westby.)

❝I always start with an art bead and design around it. Sometimes I sketch designs and have a definite plan. Other times, I let the beads lead me.❞

Sparkle and

3 Cut a 22-in. (56 cm) piece of beading wire and string 16 in. (41 cm) of coin beads and 3 and 4 mm bicones. Include a lentil bead slightly off-center. Attach each end to a textured chain end with crimp beads.

4 Cut a 17-in. (43 cm) piece of cable chain. Use jump rings (Basics) to attach each end to a textured chain end.

5 Cut a 27-in. (69 cm) piece of beading wire and string 21 in. (53 cm) of rice beads and 4 mm bicones. Use crimp beads to attach each end to a textured chain end.

necklace
1 Cut an 8-in. (20 cm) and a 14-in. (36 cm) piece of textured chain.

2 Cut an 8-in. (20 cm) piece of beading wire and string an alternating pattern of Venetian beads and 3 mm bicone crystals. On each end, string a crimp bead. Attach each end to a textured chain. Crimp the crimp beads (Basics, p. 12).

smoke

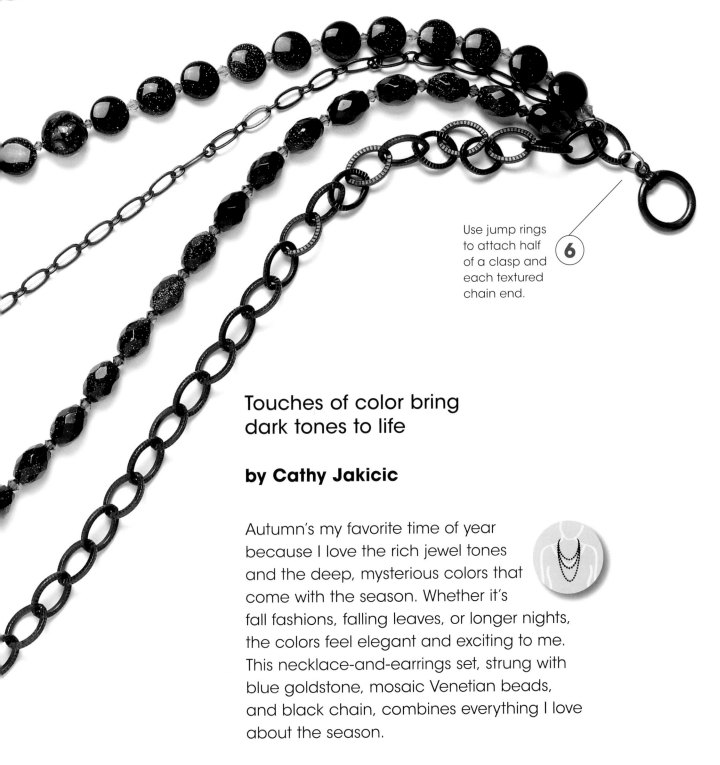

Use jump rings to attach half of a clasp and each textured chain end. **6**

Touches of color bring dark tones to life

by Cathy Jakicic

Autumn's my favorite time of year because I love the rich jewel tones and the deep, mysterious colors that come with the season. Whether it's fall fashions, falling leaves, or longer nights, the colors feel elegant and exciting to me. This necklace-and-earrings set, strung with blue goldstone, mosaic Venetian beads, and black chain, combines everything I love about the season.

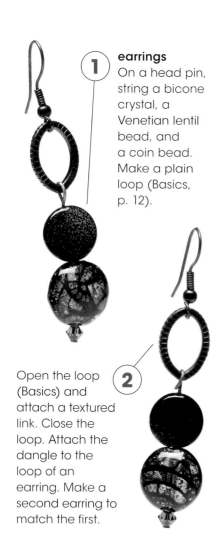

earrings

1 On a head pin, string a bicone crystal, a Venetian lentil bead, and a coin bead. Make a plain loop (Basics, p. 12).

2 Open the loop (Basics) and attach a textured link. Close the loop. Attach the dangle to the loop of an earring. Make a second earring to match the first.

Design alternative

For a look that's a little less dark, try lampworked beads from Grace Lampwork Beads, gracebeads.com, with pewter chain.

Tip

Make sure the Venetian beads on the shortest and longest strands are positioned on opposite sides of the necklace for balance.

Supplies

necklace 18–27 in. (46–69 cm)
- **3** 22 mm Venetian disk beads
- **3** 14 mm Venetian lentil beads
- **2** 8-in. (20 cm) strands 12 mm coin-shaped gemstones
- **2** 8-in. (20 cm) strands 12 mm rice-shaped gemstones
- **49–58** 4 mm bicone crystals, **35–40** color A, **14–18** color B
- **18–24** 3 mm bicone crystals, color C
- flexible beading wire, .014 or .015
- 24 in. (61 cm) textured cable chain, 17 mm links
- 17 in. (43 cm) cable chain, 7 mm links
- **4** 5–6 mm jump rings
- **6** crimp beads
- toggle clasp
- chainnose and roundnose pliers, or **2** pairs of chainnose pliers
- diagonal wire cutters

earrings
- **2** 14 mm Venetian lentil beads
- **2** 12 mm coin-shaped gemstones
- **2** 4 mm bicone crystals
- **2** links textured cable chain, 17 mm links
- **2** 2-in. (5 cm) head pins
- pair of earring wires
- chainnose and roundnose pliers
- diagonal wire cutters

❝I love the colors in the Venetian beads. They can be carnival or cathedral, depending on my mood.**❞**

Bubbles and waves

String vacation-inspired jewelry

by Jill Lindl

I made this bracelet one winter while fantasizing about a trip to anyplace watery and warm. Sometimes finishing a project becomes a challenge — not the case with this bracelet. It was a breeze to string. Visions of bronzed feet in white sand were my only distraction. String pewter seashells and see the surf as swells of seed beads flow over perfectly round pearls.

1 Cut three pieces of beading wire (Basics, p. 12). Over all three wires, string a 9 mm seashell bead. On one wire, string: bicone crystal, 6º seed bead, pearl, 6º, bicone. On each of the remaining wires, string: seven color A 11º seed beads, one color B 11º, three color C 11ºs, one color B 11º, seven color A 11ºs.

3 On each end, over all three wires, string a 6º, a crimp bead, and half of a clasp. Check the fit, and add or remove beads if necessary. Go back through the beads just strung and tighten the wires. Crimp the crimp bead (Basics) and trim the excess wire.

2 Repeat the pattern in step 1, alternating 9 mm and 13 mm seashell beads, until the strands are within 1½ in. (3.8 cm) of the finished length.

Supplies

- ◆ **2-3** 13 mm pewter seashell beads
- ◆ **3-4** 9 mm pewter seashell beads
- ◆ **4-6** 9 mm round pearls
- ◆ **8-12** 4 mm bicone crystals
- ◆ **10-14** 6º seed beads
- ◆ 2 g 11º seed beads, color A
- ◆ 1 g 11º seed beads, color B
- ◆ 1 g 11º seed beads, color C
- ◆ flexible beading wire, .014 or .015
- ◆ **2** crimp beads
- ◆ toggle clasp
- ◆ chainnose or crimping pliers
- ◆ diagonal wire cutters

Pearls

Classic
combination

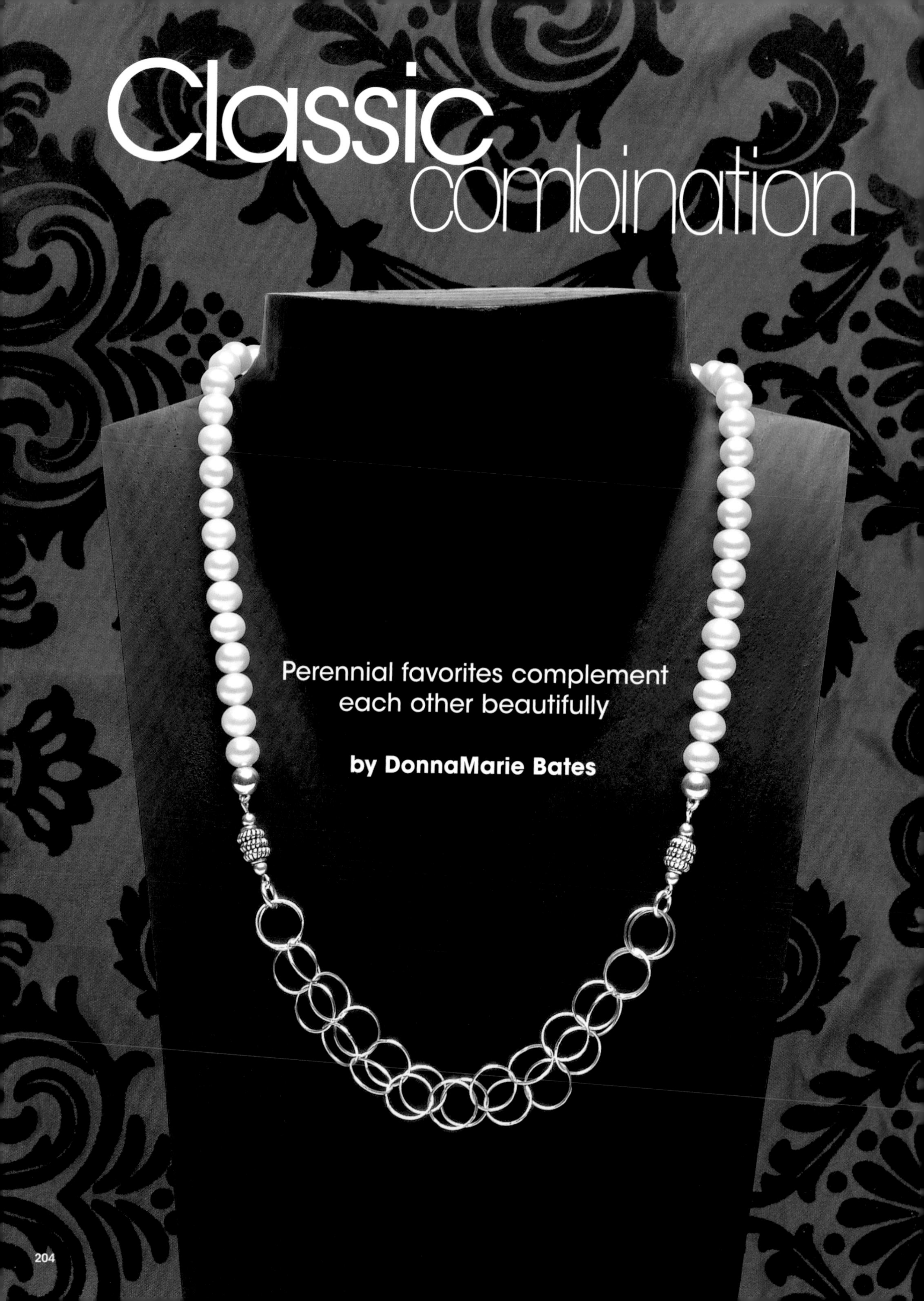

Perennial favorites complement
each other beautifully

by DonnaMarie Bates

I was working with pearls and chain independently, when one day I saw them lying next to each other — and inspiration struck. The pearls' beautiful luster, the silver's metallic shine, and the roundness of both materials make them a natural pairing. A dainty, elegant necklace and simple earrings is the result.

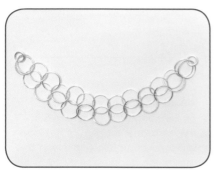

1 necklace • Cut a 9-in. (23 cm) piece of chain, making sure it has an even number of links. Fold the chain in half. On each end, open a jump ring (Basics, p. 12) and attach the two end links. Close the jump ring.

2 On an eye pin, string a 3 mm round spacer, a barrel spacer, and a 3 mm spacer. Make a plain loop (Basics) perpendicular to the first. Make a second eye pin unit. Open a loop (Basics) of each unit and attach a jump ring from step 1. Close the loop.

Supplies

necklace 18 in. (46 cm)
- 16-in. (41 cm) strand 7–8 mm freshwater pearls
- **4** 7 mm barrel spacers
- **2** 6 mm large-hole spacers
- **8** 3 mm round spacers
- flexible beading wire, .014 or .015
- 9 in. (23 cm) chain, 9–10 mm links
- **2** 1-in. (2.5 cm) eye pins
- **2** 5–6 mm jump rings
- **4** crimp beads
- toggle clasp
- ⅜ in. (10 mm) French (bullion) wire (optional)
- chainnose and roundnose pliers
- diagonal wire cutters
- crimping pliers (optional)

earrings
- **4** 7–8 mm freshwater pearls
- **4** 3 mm round spacers
- 5 in. (13 cm) chain, 9–10 mm links
- **4** 1-in. (2.5 cm) decorative head pins
- pair of lever-back earring wires
- chainnose and roundnose pliers
- diagonal wire cutters

3 Cut an 8–9-in. (20–23 cm) piece of beading wire. On one end, string a 6 mm spacer, a crimp bead, and the remaining loop of the eye pin unit. Go back through the beads just strung, tighten the wire, and crimp the crimp bead (Basics). Repeat on the other side of the chain.

4 On each wire, string: 19 to 24 pearls, 3 mm spacer, barrel spacer, 3 mm spacer, crimp bead, half of a clasp. Check the fit, and add or remove beads if necessary. Go back through the last few beads strung and tighten the wire. Crimp the crimp bead and trim the excess wire.

“What could be better than combining traditional favorites to give jewelry modern flair?”

1 earrings • On a decorative head pin, string a pearl and a 3 mm round spacer. Make the first half of a wrapped loop (Basics, p. 12). Make a second pearl unit.

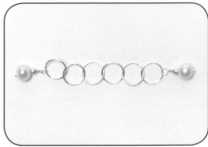

2 Cut a six-link piece of chain. On each end, attach a pearl unit and complete the wraps.

3 Open the loop of an earring wire (Basics). Attach the third link of the chain. Close the loop. Make a second earring to match.

Tips

• Before stringing a plain loop on beading wire, as in step 3 of the necklace, make sure the loop is closed completely so it won't slip off the beading wire.
• If in doubt about the loop, string about 5 mm of French wire (also called bullion) on the beading wire before going back through the last few beads. The French wire will add thickness as well as protect the beading wire from fraying.

Design alternative

Exchange off-center layered links for the centered chain. Three strands of 5 mm crystal pearls balance a short strand of 8 mms.

Knot a classic pearl
necklace in a snap

by Debbie Tuttle

Knot this time

New to knotting? You'll get into the rhythm of this knotted necklace project with just a
little practice. The knots add a bit of length, so you may want to remove beads from
opposite sides of the graduated strand before you start. (Use the leftover beads in
earrings.) Take your time tying knots; take breaks rather than trying to finish in one sitting.
If you're pressed for time, try a simpler version with bigger beads (like the ones on p. 209).

1 a necklace • Unwind a card of beading cord.
  b On the end without the needle, string a bead tip and tie two overhand knots (Basics, p. 12), one on top of the other. Trim the excess cord and apply glue to the knot.

2 a Use chainnose pliers to close the bead tip around the knot.
  b Tie an overhand knot next to the bead tip.

3 Starting from one end of a strand of graduated beads, string a bead and tie a knot. Repeat until the strand is symmetrical and within 1 in. (2.5 cm) of the finished length. End with a knot. Repeat steps 1b and 2a.

4 On each end, close the loop of the bead tip. On one end, open a jump ring (Basics). Attach a lobster claw clasp and the bead tip's loop. Close the jump ring. Repeat on the other end, substituting a soldered jump ring for the clasp.

5 Trim the head from a head pin. Make a plain loop (Basics). String a bicone crystal, a bead, and a bicone. Make a plain loop. On another head pin, string a bicone, a bead, and a bicone. Make a plain loop.

6 Open each loop (Basics) of the two-loop bead unit. Attach the head-pin unit to one loop and the soldered jump ring to the other. Close the loops.

Supplies

necklace 17½ in. (44.5 cm)
- 15–16-in. (38–41 cm) strand 3–7 mm graduated beads
- **4** 4 mm bicone crystals
- card of beading cord with attached needle, size 4
- **2** 2-in. (5 cm) head pins
- **2** 3–4 mm jump rings
- **2** bead tips
- lobster claw clasp and soldered jump ring
- chainnose and roundnose pliers
- diagonal wire cutters
- G-S Hypo Cement
- awl (optional)

bracelet
- **32–38** 3–7 mm graduated beads
- 4 mm bicone crystal
- card of beading cord with attached needle, size 4
- 1¼ in. (3.2 cm) chain, 4–6 mm links
- 2-in. (5 cm) head pin
- **2** 3–4 mm jump rings
- **2** bead tips
- lobster claw clasp
- chainnose and roundnose pliers
- diagonal wire cutters
- G-S Hypo Cement
- awl (optional)

earrings
- **6** 3–7 mm round beads, in graduated pairs
- **2** 4 mm bicone crystals
- **2** 2-in. (5 cm) head pins
- pair of earring wires
- chainnose and roundnose pliers
- diagonal wire cutters

66 Don't be afraid to try new types of projects. Have fun and wear your designs everywhere. **99**

1 bracelet • Follow steps 1 and 2 of the necklace. String three beads and tie an overhand knot (Basics, p. 12). Alternate three beads and a knot until the bracelet is within 1 in. (2.5 cm) of the finished length. End with a knot.

2 Repeat steps 1b and 2a of the necklace. On each end, close the loop of the bead tip. On one end, open a jump ring (Basics). Attach a lobster claw clasp and the bead tip's loop. Close the jump ring. Repeat on the other end, substituting a 1¼-in. (3.2 cm) piece of chain for the clasp.

3 On a head pin, string two beads and a bicone crystal. Make the first half of a wrapped loop (Basics). Attach the end link of the chain and complete the wraps.

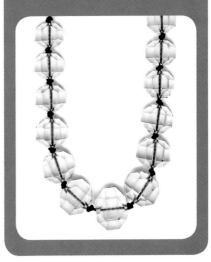

1 earrings • On a head pin, string three beads and a bicone crystal. Make a plain loop (Basics, p. 12).

2 Open the loop of an earring wire (Basics). Attach the dangle and close the loop. Make a second earring to match the first.

Speedier stringing

For a quicker project and easier knotting, use bigger beads. String the thickest beading cord that will go through the beads. (I would use size 12 for these beads.)

Tip

To accurately place knots: Use roundnose pliers or an awl to pull the knot close to the bead as you tighten it.

Design alternative

Use a strand of vintage crystals for this version. Check estate sales and antique shops for graduated crystal necklaces that you can restring. Then, knot the crystals on a colorful cord that really makes them pop.

Chained pearls

Pearls and a variety of links draw attention

by Julie Boonshaft

Classic pearls lend this bracelet a sophisticated look, while chains in several shades of silver give it mesmerizing depth. Mix bright chains with patinated silver or gunmetal so each strand has a unique identity. If there's a wedding in your future, choose pearls in the colors of your big day for instant bridesmaid jewelry.

1 On a head pin, string a 4–5 mm pearl. Make the first half of a wrapped loop (Basics, p. 12). Make seven pearl dangles.

2 Cut a 2-in. (5 cm) piece of wire and make the first half of a wrapped loop on one end. String a 4–5 mm pearl and make the first half of a wrapped loop. Make 11 4–5 mm pearl connectors and five 6–7 mm pearl connectors.

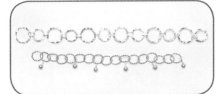

3 Cut a 7-in. (18 cm) piece of 11–13 mm link chain and a 5½-in. (14 cm) piece of 8–10 mm link chain. Attach six pearl dangles to the 8–10 mm chain. Complete the wraps as you go.

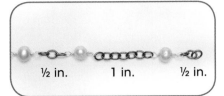

½ in.   1 in.   ½ in.

4 Cut three ½-in. (1.3 cm) and two 1-in. (2.5 cm) pieces of 4–7 mm link chain. Attach a 6–7 mm pearl connector to each end of a ½-in. (1.3 cm) chain. On each end, attach a 1-in. (2.5 cm) chain, a 6–7 mm pearl connector, and a ½-in. (1.3 cm) chain. Complete the wraps as you go.

5 Cut six ½–¾-in. (1.3–1.9 cm) pieces of 2–3 mm link chain. Use 4–5 mm pearl connectors to attach the chains.

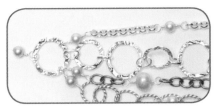

6 Use 4–5 mm pearl connectors to attach an end link of each small-link chain to an end link of the large-link chain. Attach a pearl dangle to the same link.

7 Use a 6–7 mm pearl connector to attach the other end link of the large-link chain and a lobster claw clasp. Use 4–5 mm pearl connectors to attach the end links of the small-link chains to the 6–7 mm pearl connector.

Supplies

- **5** 6–7 mm pearls
- **18** 4–5 mm pearls
- 32 in. (81 cm) 24-gauge wire
- 7 in. (18 cm) chain, 11–13 mm links
- 5½ in. (14 cm) chain, 8–10 mm links
- 4 in. (10 cm) chain, 4–7 mm links
- 5 in. (13 cm) chain, 2–3 mm links
- **7** 2-in. (5 cm) 24-gauge head pins
- 16–18 mm lobster claw clasp
- chainnose and roundnose pliers
- diagonal wire cutters

Design alternative

Too much chain for your taste? Reverse the chain-to-pearl ratio with a two-strand bracelet, a few links of chain, and pearls in similar colors.

Extend a **stranc**

String an inexpensive
alternative to a three-strand
pearl necklace

by Jane Konkel

Cultura pearls are glass beads dipped multiple times in a coating that rivals the look of real pearls. These Czech glass pearls resemble more expensive glass pearls in their consistent color and uniform size, yet are considerably less costly. The design is simple — two repeated patterns using beads in four sizes. The magnetic clasp easily allows you to wrap the long strand several times around your neck.

1 necklace • Cut a piece of beading wire (Basics, p. 12). String: 4 mm pearl, 6 mm pearl, 8 mm pearl, 10 mm pearl, 8 mm, 6 mm. Repeat the pattern three times.

2 String: four 4 mms, three 6 mms, two 8 mms, 10 mm, two 8 mms, three 6 mms. Repeat the pattern three times.

3 String three 4 mms. String the pattern in step 1 five times. String the pattern in step 2 three times. String three 4 mms. String the pattern in step 1 six times. String the pattern in step 2 twice.

4 On each end, string a crimp bead, a 4 mm, and half of a clasp. Check the fit, and add or remove beads from each end if necessary. Go back through the last few beads strung and tighten the wire. Crimp the crimp bead (Basics) and trim the excess wire.

> **❝I couldn't help but think of Mardi Gras as I strung this colorful strand.❞**

1 earrings • On a head pin, string: 10 mm pearl, 8 mm pearl, 6 mm pearl, 4 mm pearl. Make a wrapped loop (Basics, p. 12).

2 Open the loop of an earring wire (Basics) and attach the dangle. Close the loop. Make a second earring to match the first.

Tips

• This necklace wraps three times around the neck. If you would like to wrap yours four times, string each pattern two more times on each end.
• If you're not sure how long you want your necklace to be, don't cut the wire in step 1. String beads with the beading wire on the spool and decide the length as you go.

Supplies

necklace 57 in. (1.4 m)
♦ **22–30** 10 mm pearls
♦ **66–80** 8 mm pearls
♦ **84–101** 6 mm pearls
♦ **60–74** 4 mm pearls
♦ flexible beading wire, .014 or .015
♦ **2** crimp beads
♦ magnetic clasp
♦ chainnose or crimping pliers
♦ diagonal wire cutters

earrings
♦ **2** 10 mm pearls
♦ **2** 8 mm pearls
♦ **2** 6 mm pearls
♦ **2** 4 mm pearls
♦ **2** 2-in. (5 cm) head pins
♦ pair of earring wires
♦ chainnose and roundnose pliers
♦ diagonal wire cutters

Cultura Czech glass pearls and magnetic clasp from Shipwreck Beads, shipwreckbeads.com.

Design alternative

This subdued design incorporates Swarovski pearls and sterling silver bead caps.

Thanks a bunch

Pearl "grapes" make bountiful earrings

by Camilla Jorgensen

Make these lovely earrings as a gift for a friend with a passion for wine and food. Change the "vintage" and number of beads to personalize these lush earrings for any occasion.

Supplies

- **42–54** 5–6 mm button pearls
- 3 in. (7.6 cm) cable chain, 1 mm links
- **42–54** 1-in. (2.5 cm) decorative head pins
- **2** 3–4 mm jump rings
- earring posts with ear nuts
- chainnose and roundnose pliers
- diagonal wire cutters

1 On a decorative head pin, string a pearl and make a plain loop (Basics, p. 12). Make 21 to 27 pearl units.

2 Cut a 1½-in. (3.8 cm) piece of chain. Open the loop of a pearl unit (Basics) and attach an end link of the chain. Close the loop. Attach two pearl units to the next link. Repeat, alternating one and two units per link, leaving about ½ in. (1.3 cm) of the chain open at the top.

3 Open a jump ring (Basics). Attach the dangle and an earring post. Close the jump ring. Make a second earring to match the first.

Design alternative

If you want a different kind of vintage, try using old-fashioned shoe buttons instead of pearls. The buttons come with premade loops and are available from TIKA Beads and Imports, tikaimports.com.

icy lines

String stick pearls for an arctic look

by Stacy Hillmer

The moody hues of winter contrast with the brightness of a frozen landscape in this necklace-and-earrings set. Stick-pearl dangles mimic icicles while faceted amethyst gemstones brood like heavy clouds. A flurry of crystals and Czech fire-polished beads adds sparkle to this seasonal ensemble.

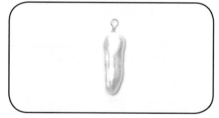

1 necklace • On a head pin, string a 22–26 mm stick pearl. Make a wrapped loop (Basics, p. 12). Make seven stick-pearl units.

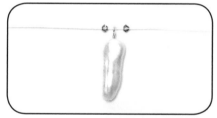

2 Cut a piece of beading wire (Basics) and center a color A bicone crystal, a stick-pearl unit, and a color A.

3 On each end, string: 17–20 mm stick pearl, 4 mm bead, 17–20 mm, color A, stick-pearl unit, color A. Repeat twice, and string a 17–20 mm.

4 On each side, string a color B bicone crystal, a 6 mm bead, a color B, and a rondelle. Repeat three times.

5 On each end, string two rondelles. String an alternating pattern of a color B and three rondelles until the strand is within 1 in. (2.5 cm) of the finished length.

6 On each end, string: color B, rondelle, crimp bead, rondelle, half of a clasp. Check the fit, and add or remove beads if necessary. Go back through the last few beads strung and tighten the wire. Crimp the crimp bead (Basics) and trim the excess wire.

1 earrings • On a head pin, string a 22–26 mm stick pearl. Make a plain loop (Basics, p. 12).

2 On an eye pin, string a 4 mm bead, a rondelle, and a 4 mm. Make a plain loop perpendicular to the first loop.

3 Open a loop (Basics) of the rondelle unit. Attach the stick-pearl unit and close the loop.

4 Open the loop of an earring wire. Attach the dangle and close the loop. Make a second earring to match the first.

Design alternative

For a dainty design, wire-wrap a neck wire, adding bicone crystals and stick-pearl dangles in random clusters.

Supplies

necklace 18 in. (46 cm)

- ◆ **7** 22–26 mm stick pearls, vertically drilled
- ◆ **14** 17–20 mm stick pearls, top drilled
- ◆ **34–42** 6 mm gemstone rondelles
- ◆ **8–10** 6 mm round Czech fire-polished beads
- ◆ **6** 4 mm round Czech glass beads
- ◆ **38–44** 3 mm bicone crystals, **14** in color A, **24–30** in color B
- ◆ flexible beading wire, .014 or .015
- ◆ **7** 2-in. (5 cm) 26-gauge head pins
- ◆ **2** crimp beads
- ◆ toggle clasp
- ◆ chainnose and roundnose pliers
- ◆ diagonal wire cutters
- ◆ crimping pliers (optional)

earrings

- ◆ **2** 22–26 mm stick pearls, vertically drilled
- ◆ **2** 6 mm gemstone rondelles
- ◆ **4** 4 mm round Czech glass beads
- ◆ **2** 2-in. (5 cm) 26-gauge head pins
- ◆ **2** 2-in. (5 cm) eye pins
- ◆ pair of earring wires
- ◆ chainnose and roundnose pliers
- ◆ diagonal wire cutters

String
unpretentious
pearls

Silk cord proves the perfect
companion for a casual look

by Irina Miech

"Finally, I'm able to string pearls on
something other than beading wire. What more
could a pearl-loving girl ask for?"

Mix silk ribbons in muted shades with pearls to make a low-key lariat. Look for pearls with 2 mm or larger holes; they'll fit the ribbons.

1 lariat • Over three ribbons, center five pearls. On each side, with all three ribbons, tie an overhand knot (Basics, p. 12) next to the end pearl.

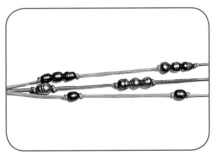

2 On each end of each ribbon, tie an overhand knot 1–3 in. (2.5–7.6 cm) from the previous knot. String one to three pearls and tie an overhand knot. Repeat.

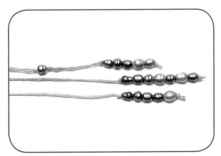

3 On one ribbon, tie an overhand knot 5–6 in. (13–15 cm) from each end. String a pearl and tie an overhand knot. Approximately 3 in. (7.6 cm) from each end of each ribbon, tie an overhand knot. String five to seven pearls and tie an overhand knot. Trim the excess ribbon.

Supplies

lariat 35 in. (89 cm)
- ◆ **65–75** 8–12 mm large-hole pearls, in four or five colors
- ◆ **3** 42-in. (1.1 m) silk ribbons, in three colors
- ◆ diagonal wire cutters

earrings
- ◆ **12** 8–12 mm large-hole pearls
- ◆ 42-in. (1.1 m) silk ribbon
- ◆ pair of earring wires
- ◆ chainnose and roundnose pliers, or **2** pairs of chainnose pliers
- ◆ diagonal wire cutters

Tip

Use a folded piece of beading wire to string the pearls on the ribbon.

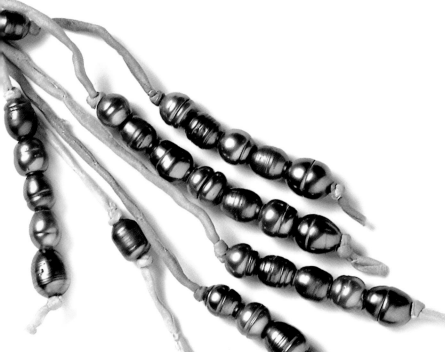

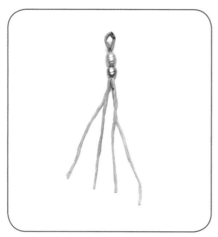

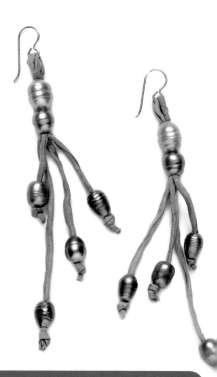

1 earrings • Cut two 5-in. (13 cm) pieces of ribbon. Fold them both in half. String two pearls over the fold (Tip, p. 219), leaving a loop above the pearls.

2 On each end, string a pearl. Tie an overhand knot (Basics, p. 12) on each end of each ribbon, staggering the placement of the knots. Trim the excess ribbon.

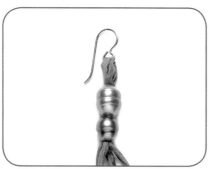

3 Open the loop of an earring wire (Basics) and attach the dangle. Make a second earring to match the first.

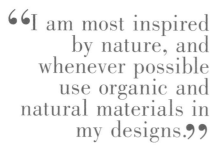

"I am most inspired by nature, and whenever possible use organic and natural materials in my designs."

Design alternative

If you don't want to invest in multiple strands of large-hole pearls, try a less expensive option. Buy two pearl strands in the same color with a variety of sizes and shapes on each.

Give the power of
power of
PINK

A necklace reminds us of
life's lessons and loops

by Miriam Fuld

The pink ribbon is worn to raise awareness about breast cancer. Make a pink-ribbon necklace with a custom-made cameo as a special tribute to the cause. During Breast Cancer Awareness Month in October, this necklace would make a wonderful gift to honor a survivor or as a remembrance of someone lost to the disease. Whether or not you stick with pink, this necklace is a great way to think through your plain loops.

1 On an eye pin, string two bicone crystals and make a plain loop (Basics, p. 12).

2 Glue a cameo to a bezel setting. Open a 4 mm jump ring (Basics) and attach the bezel and the bicone unit. Close the jump ring.

3 On an eye pin, string a bead and make a plain loop. Make 90 to 100 bead units.

4 Use 4 mm jump rings to connect a bead unit to each loop of the bicone unit. On each end, use jump rings to attach bead units until the strand is 12–16 in. (30–41 cm) long.

5 Use jump rings to connect bead units to make three more 10–14-in. (25–36 cm) strands.

6 Attach one end of each strand to a 9 mm jump ring. Repeat on the other end. If necessary, use additional 4 mm jump rings to adjust the length of each strand. If desired, twist the three short strands together before attaching.

7 Cut two 18–24-in. (46–61 cm) pieces of ribbon. String one end of a ribbon through a 9 mm jump ring. Using a needle and thread, sew the end of the ribbon to the back of the ribbon, forming a loop. Repeat on the other end.

Tips

Choose a plain loop over a wrapped loop when:
• You use 22-gauge or thicker wire.
• You use lightweight beads.
• You need to connect multiple bead units.

Supplies

necklace 24 in. (61 cm)

◆ 40 mm cameo
◆ 40 mm bezel setting
◆ **6** 16-in. (41 cm) strands 4–10 mm beads, assorted shapes
◆ **2** 4 mm bicone crystals
◆ 3–4 ft. (.9–1.2 m) ribbon
◆ **91–101** 1½-in. (3.8 cm) eye pins
◆ **2** 9 mm jump rings
◆ **90–100** 4 mm jump rings
◆ chainnose and roundnose pliers
◆ diagonal wire cutters
◆ sewing needle and thread
◆ Super New Glue

Design alternative

• Select a combination of beads in colors to match a fancy ribbon.
• Try substituting decorative bead frames for 9 mm jump rings.
• Instead of making numerous bead units, opt for beaded chain. The shortest strand has segments of beaded chain with orange rondelles.

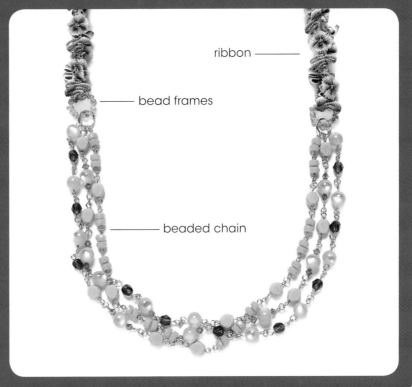

ribbon ———

——— bead frames

——— beaded chain

❝People in Israel are daring in terms of style. We wear bright mismatched colors and really long earrings.**❞**

Technique: Finishing with cones

1. On each strand, string 11º or 13º seed beads the length of a cone. (The seed beads will prevent the pearls from being pulled against the cone.) Over each pair of wires, string a cone.

2. On one side, over both wires, string: crystal, crimp bead, crystal, Wire Guardian, lobster claw clasp. Repeat on the other side, substituting a 3-in. (7.6 cm) chain for the clasp. Check the fit, and add or remove beads if necessary. With each pair of wires, go back through the beads just strung. Tighten the wires.

3. On each side, crimp the crimp bead (Basics) and trim the excess wire. (Note: For a neater finish, string the excess wire back through the cone.) Close a crimp cover over the finished crimp.

Repeat step 2 on the other end, substituting a 4-in. (10 cm) piece of chain for the clasp. Before crimping, check the fit and add or remove beads if necessary. Close crimp covers over the finished crimps.

③

②

Cut a 10-in. (25 cm) piece of beading wire. String pearls interspersed with crystals until the strand is half the finished length.

On one end, string: crystal, crimp bead, crystal, Wire Guardian, lobster claw clasp. Go back through the beads just strung, tighten the wire, and crimp the crimp bead (Basics, p. 12). Trim the excess wire.

①

curved-wire earrings • For each earring: On a 3-in. (7.6 cm) piece of wire, string a pearl. Make a set of wraps above it (Basics, p. 12). Make the first half of a wrapped loop (Basics). Attach the loop of an earring wire and complete the wraps.

three-pearl earrings • For each earring: On a 4-in. (10 cm) piece of wire, string three pearls. Make a set of wraps above the pearls (Basics, p. 12). Make the first half of a wrapped loop (Basics). Attach the loop of an earring post and complete the wraps.

Supplies

necklace 17 in. (43 cm)
- **2** 16-in. (41 cm) strands 14–15 mm keshi pearls, top drilled
- **20-30** 4 mm crystals
- 1 g 11º or 13º seed beads
- flexible beading wire, .010 or .012
- 2-in. (5 cm) head pin
- **2** cones
- **2** crimp beads
- **2** crimp covers
- **2** Wire Guardians
- lobster claw clasp
- 3 in. (7.6 cm) chain for extender, 8–13 mm links
- chainnose and roundnose pliers
- diagonal wire cutters
- crimping pliers (optional)

bracelet
- **10-15** 14–15 mm keshi pearls, top drilled, left over from necklace
- **7-10** 4 mm crystals
- flexible beading wire, .014 or .015
- 3–4 in. (7.6-10 cm) chain, 8–13 mm links
- **2** crimp beads
- **2** crimp covers
- **2** Wire Guardians
- lobster claw clasp
- chainnose or crimping pliers
- diagonal wire cutters

curved-wire earrings
- **2** 14–15 mm keshi pearls, top drilled, left over from necklace
- 6 in. (15 cm) 26-gauge wire
- pair of 44 mm textured earring wires
- chainnose and roundnose pliers
- diagonal wire cutters

three-pearl earrings
- **6** 14–15 mm keshi pearls, top drilled, left over from necklace
- 8 in. (20 cm) 26-gauge wire
- pair of earring posts with ear nuts
- chainnose and roundnose pliers
- diagonal wire cutters

Pearls from Lucky Gems & Jewelry Factory, luckygems.us. Textured earring wires from Fusion Beads, fusionbeads.com.

Glass and

ceramic

Inspired

An organic look is guided by a treasure of pebbles

by Melissa Cable

The Czech lampworked beads in this necklace reminded me of the pebbles I once fished out of a stream. They looked beautiful under water, but by the time I got them home, they dried and were not nearly as pretty. Though the dried pebbles ended up in the front flower bed, it was worth the effort to carry them around; the originals inspired me to make this great necklace.

1 On a head pin, string a color A bicone crystal and make a plain loop (Basics, p. 12). On another head pin, string a color B bicone, a spacer, and a color C bicone. Make a plain loop. On a third head pin, string a color D bicone and make a plain loop. Make five of each type of bead unit.

2 Cut a 2-in. (5 cm) piece of wire. Make a plain loop on one end. String a nugget and make a plain loop. Make six or seven nugget units.

3 Center a metal bead on a cord. On each side, tie an overhand knot (Basics).

4 On one end, string each loop of a nugget unit, then go through each loop again.

oy riverstones

5 Tie an overhand knot. String a lampworked bead and tie an overhand knot. Repeat the pattern in steps 3–5 two or three times.

6 On the other end, string a lampworked bead and tie an overhand knot. String a nugget as in step 4 and tie an overhand knot. String a metal bead and tie an overhand knot. Repeat two or three times.

7 Open a jump ring (Basics). Attach one of each type of bead unit from step 1 and the silk cord as shown. Close the jump ring. Use jump rings to attach the remaining bead units.

8 On each end, string half of a clasp and tie two overhand knots. Use chainnose pliers to close a crimp cover over each knot.

❝I tend to like organic designs with lots of texture. I love to combine pearls and unfaceted, opaque semiprecious stones, and then throw in a pop of color and light.❞

Supplies

necklace 18 in. (46 cm)
- ◆ **6–7** 18 mm nuggets
- ◆ **6–7** 17 mm lampworked beads
- ◆ **5–7** 10 mm metal beads
- ◆ **20** 4 mm bicone crystals, in four colors
- ◆ **5** 5–7 mm spacers
- ◆ 24–28 in. (61–71 cm) silk cord
- ◆ 12–14 in. (30–36 cm) 22-gauge half-hard wire
- ◆ **15** 1½-in. (3.8 cm) head pins
- ◆ **5** 5 mm jump rings
- ◆ **2** crimp covers
- ◆ toggle clasp
- ◆ chainnose and roundnose pliers
- ◆ diagonal wire cutters

Design alternatives

- Try other lampworked beads in your design. The swirl beads in the earrings on this page and the bee and dragonfly beads were made by Kerri Fuhr, kerrifuhr.com.
- The torchworked beads below are similar in size and shape to the ones used in the original design. They were made by Stacy Frost, stacyfrost.com.

Tips

- To string the beads more easily, sew a needle to the end of the silk cord. You can also sew closed the loop on each end of the cord instead of tying knots. Use crimp covers to cover the stitches.
- I started my necklace in the center, but you can work from one end to the other if you like.

Two of Kerri Fuhr's beads make swirly earrings.

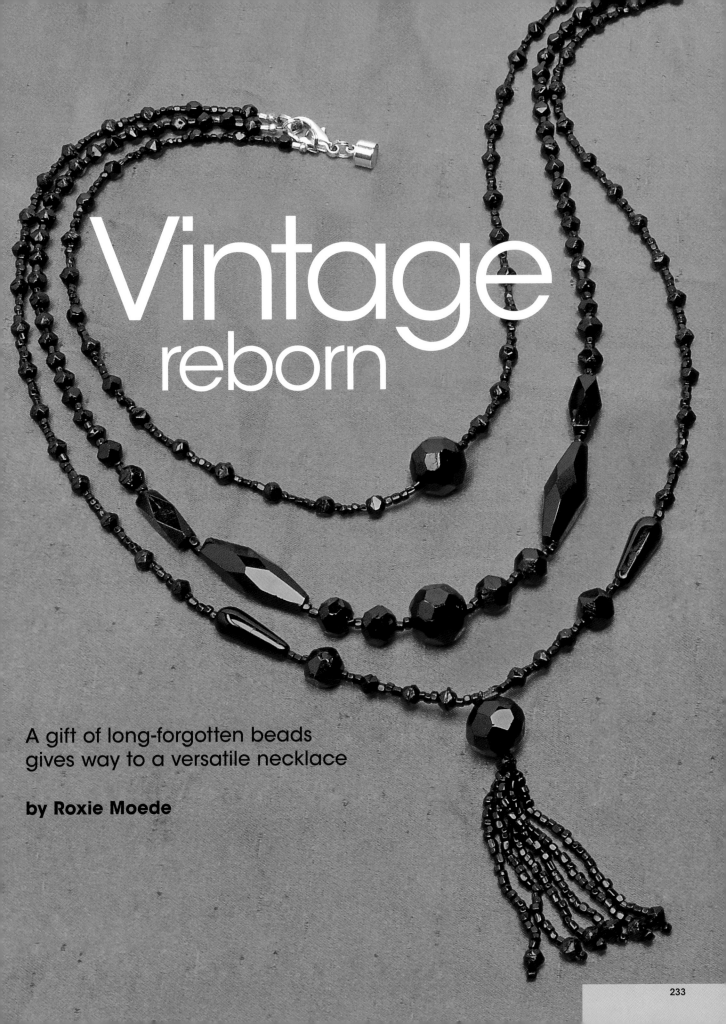

Vintage
reborn

A gift of long-forgotten beads
gives way to a versatile necklace

by Roxie Moede

My friend found these black beads in bags and bottles at an estate sale during the early '60s. Can you believe they sat on a shelf until now? If you like the vintage touch, look for similar crystals in jet, or opt for pristine crystal AB. Make a necklace, or two, or three. Each strand is detachable, so you can wear as many or as few strands as you wish.

Supplies

necklace 23 in. (58 cm)
- **2** 18 or 28 mm crystals
- **4** 15 mm bicone crystals
- **2** 14 mm round crystals
- 12 mm round crystal
- **6** 8 mm round crystals
- **80–110** 6 mm round crystals
- **6** 4 mm bicone or round crystals
- 4 g 9° seed beads
- **6** 3 mm round spacers
- flexible beading wire, .014 or .015
- **8** 6 mm split rings
- **13** crimp beads
- **2** lobster claw clasps
- magnetic clasp
- chainnose or crimping pliers
- diagonal wire cutters
- split-ring pliers (optional)

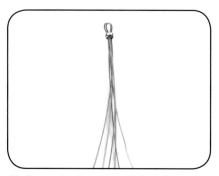

1 To make the tassel: Cut three 10-in. (25 cm) pieces of beading wire. Fold the wires in half and string a crimp bead over all six ends, leaving a ⅛-in. (3 mm) loop. Crimp the crimp bead (Basics, p. 12).

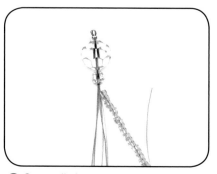

2 Over all six ends, string a 14 mm crystal and a 6 mm crystal. On one end, string: 2 in. (5 cm) of 9° seed beads, crimp bead, 4 mm crystal, 9°. Go back through the 4 mm, the crimp bead, and a few 9°s. Tighten the wire, crimp the crimp bead, and trim the excess wire. Repeat on the remaining ends.

Tip

Large bicone crystals, like the 15 mm crystals used in step 7 of this necklace, are sometimes called double-cone crystals.

> **"**I have been beading for about three years now and I just can't get enough. I have so many completed pieces, because I just bead to bead.**"**

3 Cut a piece of beading wire (Basics) for the shortest strand of your necklace. Cut two more pieces, each 4 in. (10 cm) longer than the previous piece. On the shortest wire, center a 12 mm crystal.

On each end, string five 9°s and a 6 mm. Repeat until the strand is within 2 in. (5 cm) of the finished length. End with a 6 mm.

4 On the middle wire, center a 14 mm. On each end, string: two 9°s, 8 mm crystal, two 9°s, 8 mm, two 9°s, 18 or 28 mm crystal, two 9°s, 15 mm crystal, two 9°s, 6 mm, two 9°s, 6 mm.

5 On each end of the middle strand, string a 9º and a 6 mm. Repeat until the strand is within 2 in. (5 cm) of the finished length. End with a 6 mm.

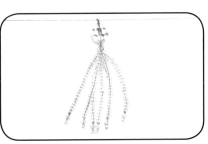

6 On the longest wire, center the tassel.

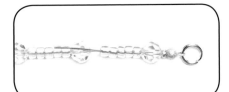

7 On each end of the longest strand, string: three 9ºs, 6 mm, three 9ºs, 6 mm, three 9ºs, 6 mm, three 9ºs, 8 mm, three 9ºs, 15 mm.

8 On each end, string five 9ºs and a 6 mm. Repeat until the strand is within 2 in. (5 cm) of the finished length. End with a 6 mm.

9 On each end of each strand, string a crimp bead, a spacer, and a split ring. Check the fit, and add or remove beads from each end if necessary. Go back through the last few beads strung and tighten the wire. Crimp the crimp bead and trim the excess wire.

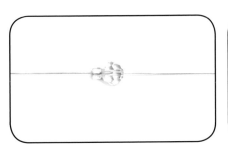

10 On each end, open the split ring (Basics) and attach a lobster claw clasp and half of a magnetic clasp.

Design alternative

If you are sure this necklace will be worn strictly as three strands, skip the lobster claw clasps. Just finish your necklace by attaching half of a clasp to the three strands on each side.

Diagonally drilled pearls point the way to a stylish set.

Keep things steady with pewter components

by Irina Miech

Form & function align
impeccably

TierraCast bead aligners allow you to string large-hole lampworked beads next to small-hole pearls with no wobble. This new finding opens up a whole new world of inspiring design opportunities.

Supplies

necklace (blue 16 in./41 cm; gold 18 in./46 cm)
- ◆ **3** 14 mm lampworked beads
- ◆ **16-in.** (41 cm) strand 6 mm pearls, diagonally drilled
- ◆ **6** 8 mm bead aligners
- ◆ **4** 4 mm spacers
- ◆ flexible beading wire, .014 or .015
- ◆ **2** crimp beads
- ◆ **2** crimp covers (optional)
- ◆ toggle clasp
- ◆ crimping pliers
- ◆ diagonal wire cutters

bracelet
- ◆ **2** 14 mm lampworked beads
- ◆ **28–34** 6 mm pearls, diagonally drilled
- ◆ **4** 8 mm bead aligners
- ◆ **4** 4 mm spacers
- ◆ flexible beading wire, .014 or .015
- ◆ **2** crimp beads
- ◆ **2** crimp covers (optional)
- ◆ toggle clasp
- ◆ crimping pliers
- ◆ diagonal wire cutters

1 necklace • Cut a piece of beading wire (Basics, p. 12). Center a bead aligner, a 14 mm bead, and an aligner.

2 On each end, string five pearls, an aligner, a 14 mm, and an aligner.

On each end, string pearls until the strand is within 1 in. (2.5 cm) of the finished length.

3 On each end, string a spacer, a crimp bead, a spacer, and half of a clasp. Check the fit, and add or remove beads if necessary. Go back through the beads just strung and tighten the wire. Make a folded crimp (Basics) and trim the excess wire. If desired, close a crimp cover over each crimp.

Tip

Use the outer notch of your crimping pliers to gently close a crimp cover over each folded crimp.

1 bracelet • Cut a piece of beading wire (Basics, p. 12). Center 4–6 in. (10–15 cm) of pearls.

2 On each end, string a bead aligner, a 14 mm bead, and an aligner. Follow step 3 of the necklace to finish.

Design alternative

Use 9 mm and 11 mm lampwork beads as the focal points of this necklace. The copper bead aligners and burgundy stick pearls complement the lampwork beads. Beads by Jeff Plath available at Eclectica, 262.641.0910, and Glass River Beads, glassriverbeads.com.

An etched
copper pendant
falls from a
moonlit sky

by Lorelei Eurto

Starry night

I was playing around with Jennifer Stumpf's etched copper pendant and realized the holes lined up perfectly with the holes of Heather Powers' Starry Night cuff bead. A few colorful drops, rounds, and rondelles mimic the night sky filled with swirling clouds, blazing stars, and the bright moon of Van Gogh's masterpiece. A pair of polymer clay disk earrings is an easy, artsy addition.

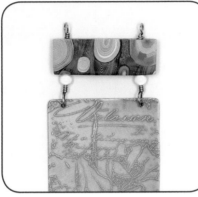

1 necklace • Cut two 3-in. (7.6 cm) pieces of wire. On one end of each wire, make the first half of a wrapped loop (Basics, p. 12). Attach a corner hole of the pendant and complete the wraps.

2 On each wire, string a 4 mm bead and an outer hole of a cuff bead. Make a wrapped loop.

3 Cut a 4-in. (10 cm) piece of wire and make a wrapped loop. String: loop of the cuff bead, 4 mm, tube bead (Tip, p. 240), 4 mm, remaining loop of the cuff bead. Make a wrapped loop.

4 Cut 10 or 12 ½–2½-in. (1.3–6.4 cm) pieces of chain.
Open the link (Basics) of a short piece of chain and attach a loop of the tube unit. Close the link. Repeat on the other side.

Supplies

necklace 21 in. (53 cm)
- 42 mm etched copper pendant with three holes (Jennifer Stumpf, jenniferstumpf.etsy.com)
- 36 mm Starry Night cuff bead (Heather Powers, humblebeads.com)
- 18–30 mm tube bead
- 12–18 mm charm and jump ring
- **4** 10 mm boro glass beads (Unicorne Beads, unicornebeads.com)
- **14–18** 4–8 mm beads
- 34–40 in. (86–100 cm) 22-gauge Artistic Wire
- 14–18 in. (36–46 cm) chain, 3 mm links
- 14 mm hook-and-eye clasp
- chainnose and roundnose pliers
- diagonal wire cutters

earrings
- **2** 10 mm Starry Night disk beads (Heather Powers)
- **2** 18–30 mm tube beads
- **2** 4 mm bicone crystals
- **2** ½-in. (1.3 cm) head pins
- **2** 2-in. (5 cm) eye pins
- pair of earring wires
- chainnose and roundnose pliers
- diagonal wire cutters

"Sometimes I sit down at my beading table with no ideas. I just let myself try out different bead combinations and it usually snowballs from there."

5 Cut a 3-in. (7.6 cm) piece of wire and make a wrapped loop. String one to four beads and make a wrapped loop. Make eight to 10 bead units.

6 On each side, open the end link of the chain and attach a bead unit. Close the link. Continue attaching chains and bead units until your necklace is within ½ in. (1.3 cm) of the finished length.

7 Check the fit, and trim chain from each end if necessary. On each end, attach half of a clasp.
Open a jump ring (Basics) and attach a charm and the bottom hole of the pendant. Close the jump ring.

1 earrings • On a head pin, string a disk bead. Make a plain loop (Basics, p. 12).

2 On an eye pin, string a bicone crystal and a tube bead. Make a plain loop.

3 Open the loop of the disk unit (Basics) and attach a loop of the tube unit. Close the loop.

4 Open the loop of an earring wire, attach the dangle, and close the loop. Make a second earring to match the first.

Design alternative

For this necklace, pair a brass etched pendant with cuff and disk beads inspired by Claude Monet. You can opt for fancy copper and brass chain instead of attaching bead units to links of chain.

Tip

For the necklace, choose a tube bead that is the approximate length of your cuff bead (30 mm). If you choose a shorter tube, string beads on each end of the tube in step 2 to make up the difference.

Tie up
loose ends

Finish a recycled-glass bracelet with a loop of waxed linen cord

by Brenda Schweder

This down-to-earth bracelet features a variety of recycled-glass beads from Ghana. The glass snake beads (also from Africa) link together like the vertebrae of a snake. The unusual linen loop closure is the perfect finishing touch.

1 If using a charm with a loop, go to step 2. On a head pin, string a 25 mm metal bead. Make a wrapped loop (Basics, p. 12). Set the bead unit aside for step 6.

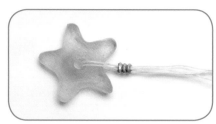

2 Cut two 36-in. (.9 m) pieces of waxed linen cord. Center a star pendant over the cords. Over all four ends, string three spacers.

3 String: snake bead, round bead, spacer, round, spacer, round, spacer.

4 String: tube bead, spacer, round, snake bead, barrel bead, spacer, barrel, spacer.

5 String: round, spacer, round, spacer, barrel, snake bead, barrel, spacer.

6 String: round, snake bead, barrel, charm or bead unit from step 1, 7–8 mm metal bead.

Supplies

- 30 mm recycled-glass star pendant (eShopAfrica.com)
- 28–30 mm recycled-glass tube
- **7** 12–16 mm recycled-glass rounds
- **5** 8–12 mm recycled-glass barrels
- **3** 9 mm snake beads
- 7–8 mm metal bead
- **12** 4 mm spacers
- 20–30 mm charm with loop, or 25 mm metal bead with 2-in. (5 cm) head pin
- 6 ft. (1.8 m) waxed linen cord (Sun Country Gems, suncountrygems.com)
- chainnose and roundnose pliers
- diagonal wire cutters
- G-S Hypo Cement
- large-eye sewing needle

Recycled-glass beads from Happy Mango Beads, happymangobeads.com.

"Wrapping the cord to make this loop reminds me of the *throw* method of knitting."

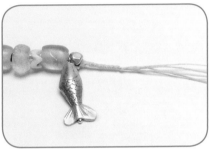

7 To make a loop closure: Separate the cords into two pairs. Tie a surgeon's knot (Basics) next to the 7 mm bead. Separate the cords into a group of three filler cords and a single cord.

8 Wrap the single cord snugly around the three filler cords. After about 20 wraps, regroup the cords and pick up the longest one to use as the wrapping cord. Repeat until you've made a loop large enough to accommodate the star pendant.

9 Thread one end through the eye of a needle. Position the needle parallel to the wrapped cord, and wrap one cord several times around the wrapped cord and the needle.

10 Hold the wraps securely while pulling the needle through the center. Tie a surgeon's knot with the wrapping cord and the two adjacent cords. Apply glue to the knot. Trim the excess cord as desired.

Tips

• Look for G-S Hypo Cement with a precision applicator. The applicator allows you to place small amounts of glue without creating a mess, and it eliminates waste.
• If this is your first time working with waxed linen cord, you are going to get hooked quickly. The cord comes in a full array of colors, you can twist the ends to fit multiple strands through beads, and its tacky texture makes it easy to wrap a coiled loop or tie decorative knots.

Design alternative

In this bracelet, I used recycled-glass beads, brown glass snake beads, a Tibetan engraved brass bicone, a brass and pewter Egyptian cat pendant, and a double dorje pendant made of copper, brass, and pewter. Supplies from Happy Mango Beads, happymangobeads.com.

Golden tones

Bring harmony to
repeating elements

by Helene Tsigistras

Repetition is the theme of this jewelry set. Golden tones and textured swirls are replicated in various proportions throughout the design. When choosing links, look for designs to complement the pattern and colors in the ceramic beads.

1 necklace • On a head pin, string a spacer and a 20 mm bead. Make the first half of a wrapped loop (Basics, p. 12). Attach one loop of a link and complete the wraps. Set aside for step 9.

2 Cut a 3-in. (7.6 cm) piece of wire. Make the first half of a wrapped loop on one end. String six spacers, a round bead, and six spacers. Make the first half of a wrapped loop. Make four spacer units.

3 Cut a 3-in. (7.6 cm) piece of wire. Make the first half of a wrapped loop on one end. String a 20 mm bead. Make the first half of a wrapped loop. Make four 20 mm units.

4 Attach one loop of a spacer unit to a soldered jump ring. Attach the other loop to one loop of a link. Complete the wraps.

5a Attach: 20 mm unit, link, spacer unit, link, 20 mm unit. Complete the wraps as you go.
  b Repeat steps 4 and 5a on the other side of the soldered jump ring.

6 Cut two 8–12-in. (20–30 cm) pieces of beading wire. On one end of each wire, string a crimp bead and the end loop of a 20 mm unit. Go back through the crimp bead and tighten the wire. Crimp the crimp bead (Basics).

7 On each wire, string six spacers and a round bead. String spacers until the strands are within 2 in. (5 cm) of the finished length.

8 On one wire, string a crimp bead and a hook clasp. On the other wire, string a crimp bead and a soldered jump ring. Check the fit, and add or remove spacers if necessary. Go back through the last few beads strung and tighten the wires. Crimp the crimp beads and trim the excess wire.

9 Use a split ring (Basics) to attach the dangle from step 1 and the center soldered jump ring.

1 bracelet • Repeat necklace step 3 to make three or four 20 mm units. Attach 20 mm units and links until the bracelet is within 2 in. (5 cm) of the finished length.

2 Open a jump ring (Basics, p. 12) and attach a hook clasp to one end. On the other end, attach a split ring or use another jump ring to attach a soldered jump ring.

1 earrings • On a head pin, string a bead cap, a round bead, a cone, and a spacer. Make a wrapped loop (Basics, p. 12).

2 Open the loop of an earring wire (Basics). Attach the dangle and close the loop. Make a second earring to match the first.

Design alternative

Simplify this version by skipping the round beads and 4 mm spacers. You can also opt for a cooler palette mixed with silver.

Supplies

necklace 23 in. (58 cm)

- ◆ **5** 20 mm ceramic beads
- ◆ **6** 10 mm round ceramic beads
- ◆ **150–180** 4 mm flat spacers
- ◆ flexible beading wire, .014 or .015
- ◆ 24 in. (61 cm) 22-gauge half-hard wire
- ◆ **7** 26 mm links with two loops
- ◆ 2-in. (5 cm) head pin
- ◆ **2** 9 mm soldered jump rings
- ◆ split ring
- ◆ **4** crimp beads
- ◆ hook clasp with jump ring
- ◆ chainnose and roundnose pliers
- ◆ diagonal wire cutters
- ◆ crimping pliers (optional)
- ◆ split-ring pliers (optional)

bracelet

- ◆ **3–4** 20 mm ceramic beads
- ◆ 9–12 in. (23–30 cm) 22-gauge half-hard wire
- ◆ **4–5** 26 mm links with two loops
- ◆ **1–2** 5 mm jump rings
- ◆ hook clasp and soldered jump ring or split ring
- ◆ chainnose and roundnose pliers
- ◆ diagonal wire cutters
- ◆ split-ring pliers (optional)

earrings

- ◆ **2** 10 mm round ceramic beads
- ◆ **2** 4 mm flat spacers
- ◆ **2** 6 mm bead caps
- ◆ **2** 2-in. (5 cm) head pins
- ◆ **2** 10 mm cones
- ◆ pair of earring wires
- ◆ chainnose and roundnose pliers
- ◆ diagonal wire cutters

Urban attitude

Silver bead frames mimic the shape of beads while cradling AB crystals for a modern look

by Sue Godfrey

This bracelet features Czech glass beads that are perfect for any city slicker. "Oil drops" on a black background form a street-smart rainbow, while windows of blue and yellow reflect the sky of a dusky cityscape.

1 Cut a piece of beading wire (Basics, p. 12). String: saucer spacer, Czech glass bead, saucer, liquid-silver tube, one hole of a bead frame, round spacer, bicone, round, other hole of the bead frame, tube.

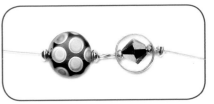

2 Repeat the pattern until the strand is within 1 in. (2.5 cm) of the finished length. Substitute a saucer for the final tube.

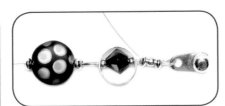

3 On each end, string a crimp bead, a saucer, and half of a clasp. Check the fit, and add or remove beads if necessary. Go back through the last few beads strung and tighten the wire. Crimp the crimp bead (Basics) and trim the excess wire.

Supplies

- ◆ **5–6** 10 mm Czech glass beads
- ◆ **5** 9 mm circle bead frames
- ◆ **5** 6 mm bicone crystals
- ◆ **10–11** 4 mm twisted liquid-silver tube beads
- ◆ **13** 3 mm saucer spacers
- ◆ **10** 2 mm round spacers
- ◆ flexible beading wire, .014 or .015
- ◆ **2** crimp beads
- ◆ snap clasp
- ◆ chainnose or crimping pliers
- ◆ diagonal wire cutters

Stroke of genius

Brushstroke-shaped crystals inspire design

by Linda Arline Hartung

As soon as I saw the curves of these crystals, I thought of the brushwork of impressionists such as Monet, Renoir, and Degas. The brushstroke-shaped crystals (CRYSTALLIZED™ – *Swarovski Elements* calls them aquiline) come top- or center-drilled, but the options aren't available in all colors and sizes. The trick is to organize your shopping. Check availability, plan the jewelry bead by bead, make a list, and then shop.

Assembling a clasp

- 8 mm crystal teardrop flat back #4300
- **2** 8 mm crystal oval flat backs or navettes #4200
- **2** 5 mm crystal flat back rhinestones #1028
- two-part epoxy
- tweezers or a toothpick with a bit of museum putty

Apply two-part epoxy to the inside of each bezel. Set the crystal, making sure it is level. Let dry.

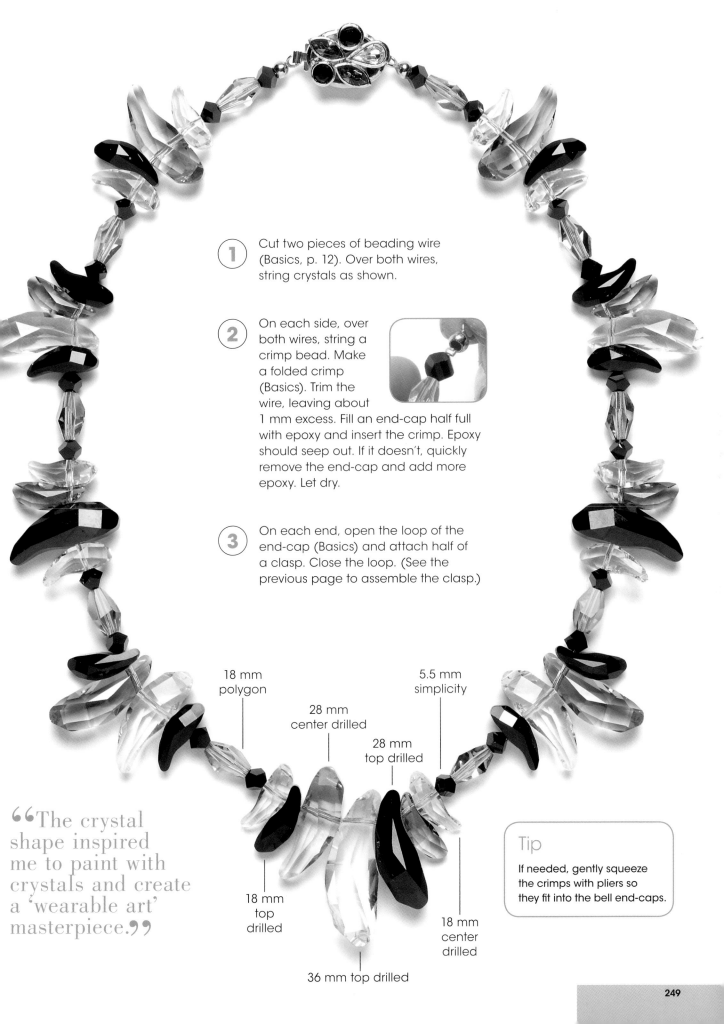

1 Cut two pieces of beading wire (Basics, p. 12). Over both wires, string crystals as shown.

2 On each side, over both wires, string a crimp bead. Make a folded crimp (Basics). Trim the wire, leaving about 1 mm excess. Fill an end-cap half full with epoxy and insert the crimp. Epoxy should seep out. If it doesn't, quickly remove the end-cap and add more epoxy. Let dry.

3 On each end, open the loop of the end-cap (Basics) and attach half of a clasp. Close the loop. (See the previous page to assemble the clasp.)

18 mm polygon

28 mm center drilled

28 mm top drilled

5.5 mm simplicity

18 mm top drilled

18 mm center drilled

36 mm top drilled

"The crystal shape inspired me to paint with crystals and create a 'wearable art' masterpiece.**"**

Tip

If needed, gently squeeze the crimps with pliers so they fit into the bell end-caps.

Supplies

necklace 19 in. (48 cm)
- ◆ 36 mm aquiline crystal, top drilled, color A
- ◆ **5** 28 mm aquiline crystals, top drilled, **2** color A, **2** color B, **1** color C
- ◆ **7** 28 mm aquiline crystals, center drilled, **2** color A, **3** color B, **2** color C
- ◆ **10** 18 mm aquiline crystals, top drilled, **5** color B, **5** color C
- ◆ **16** 18 mm aquiline crystals, center drilled, **10** color A, **6** color C
- ◆ **10** 18 mm polygon crystals, color A
- ◆ **20** 5.5 mm simplicity crystals, color C
- ◆ flexible beading wire, .018 or .019
- ◆ **2** crimp beads
- ◆ **2** 4 mm bell end-caps
- ◆ box clasp
- ◆ chainnose and roundnose pliers, or **2** pairs of chainnose pliers
- ◆ crimping pliers
- ◆ diagonal wire cutters
- ◆ two-part epoxy

bracelet
- ◆ **12** 18 mm aquiline crystals, top drilled, **3** color A, **6** color B, **3** color C
- ◆ **12** 18 mm aquiline crystals, center drilled, **6** color A, **6** color C
- ◆ **7** 5.5 mm simplicity crystals, color C
- ◆ flexible beading wire, .018 or .019
- ◆ **2** crimp beads
- ◆ **2** 4 mm bell end-caps
- ◆ box clasp
- ◆ chainnose and roundnose pliers, or **2** pairs of chainnose pliers
- ◆ crimping pliers
- ◆ diagonal wire cutters
- ◆ two-part epoxy

Tips

• Think like an impressionist in terms of light and color.

CRYSTALLIZED colors:
black and white:
    Color A: crystal
    Color B: black diamond
    Color C: jet

blue and green:
    Color A: crystal
    Color B: aquamarine
    Color C: olivine

• One strand of .024 beading wire can be substituted for two strands of .018 or .019.
• Don't substitute bicones for the simplicity crystals. You'll lose the snug fit the simplicity shape gives.

Design alternative

You can string fewer crystals if you knot and braid four coordinating strands of WireLace.

Warm pendant meets cool lampwork

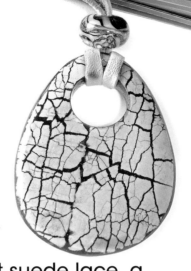

Hung from leather cord or soft suede lace, a reversible pendant is earth-friendly and elegant

by Jane Konkel

These laminated pendants are inlaid with leaves, seed pods, and even eel skin. Resourceful artists work with industries to repurpose what would otherwise go to waste. The organic material in these pendants was obtained through recycling and was inspected by the United States Fish and Wildlife Department before entering the U.S. Pair one of these two-sided pendants with gorgeous lampworked beads.

1 Cut two 20–28-in. (51–71 cm) pieces of leather cord. To tie a lark's head knot: Fold the cords in half. Center a pendant over the fold and pull the ends through the loop.

2 Over all four ends, string a lampwork bead. Pull the bead down next to the knot.

3 On each side, position two cord ends in a crimp end. Make a folded crimp end (Basics, p. 12). Trim the excess cord.

4 On one end, open a jump ring (Basics) or chain link. Attach the loop of the crimp end and a lobster claw clasp. Close the jump ring. Repeat on the other side, substituting a jump ring or a 1-in. (2.5 cm) piece of chain for the clasp.

Supplies

necklace 24 in. (61 cm)

- 76 mm reversible pendant (coolearthwear.com)
- 21 mm large-hole lampwork bead
- 40–56 in. (1–1.4 m) 1–2 mm round leather cord
- 4 9 mm oval jump rings, or 1½ in. (3.8 cm) chain, 9 mm links
- 2 crimp ends
- lobster claw clasp
- chainnose and round-nose pliers, or 2 pairs of chainnose pliers
- diagonal wire cutters

Contributors

Lori Anderson, a full-time jewelry artist, works in Easton, Md. Contact her at lori@lorianderson.net or via her Web site, lorianderson.net.

As a world traveler, **Rupa Balachandar** likes to create jewelry that makes a statement. She regularly travels through Asia looking for components to make her jewelry and is pleased to share her finds through her Web site, rupab.com. Contact her via e-mail at info@rupab.com.

DonnaMarie Bates, owner of Jewelry by DonnaMarie, is a jewelry designer in upstate New York. Her custom pieces have fashion-forward sensibility and offer a sense of individual and personal style very much in demand by women today; contact her at jewelrybydonnamarie.com.

Contact **Julie Boonshaft** via e-mail at julie@julieboonshaftjewelry.com, or visit julieboonshaftjewelry.com.

Melissa Cable owns beadclub bead store in Woodinville, Wash., where she enjoys teaching students of all levels. She can be reached at melissa@beadclub.com or by visiting www.beadclub.com.

Maria Camera co-owns Bella Bella! in Milwaukee, Wis. Contact her in care of Kalmbach books.

Rebecca Conrad-LaMere is always looking for new design inspirations. Contact her at bjc1941@aol.com.

Nina Cooper and her team at Nina Designs create gorgeous charms, beads and findings from sterling silver. She brings 25 years of experience and passion to every design. Contact her at ninadesigns.com.

Jess DiMeo teaches at Turquoise-Stringbeads in Fall River, Mass. Contact her via e-mail at turq2000@turquoise-stringbeads.com.

Contact **Erin Dolan** in care of Kalmbach books.

Surrounded and inspired by artwork while working her day job at a museum, **Lorelei Eurto** is a self-taught jewelry designer. Visit www.Lorelei1141.etsy.com, and read more about her process of creating fun. practical, easy-to-wear jewelry at her blog, http://Lorelei1141.blogspot.com.

Contact **Laurie Feldman** via e-mail at laurief1956@earthlink.net

Naomi Fujimoto is Senior Editor of *BeadStyle* magazine and the author of *Cool Jewels: Beading Projects for Teens*. Visit her blog at cooljewelsnaomi.blogspot.com, or contact her in care of *BeadStyle*.

Miriam Fuld is a stay-at-home mom, artist, and jewelry designer. Contact her at mim@mimzdesign.com or visit her Web site, www.mimzdesign.com.

Sue Godfrey is a part-time jewelry artist who lives in Waukesha, Wis., with her husband and two kids. She is also an instructor for Midwest Beads in Brookfield, Wis. Contact her via email at sggodfrey@wi.rr.com.

Contact **Mia Gofar** via e-mail at mia@miagofar.com or her Web site at miagofar.com.

Jennifer Gorski creates jewelry from her home in the Rocky Mountains of Colorado. Jewelry inspirations often come to her in the middle of the night while she's sleeping. Contact Jennifer at djgorski@comcast.net.

Rebekah Gough is a jewelry artist who works from her home studio in Seattle, Wash., where she lives with her husband and two little boys. Contact her at rebekah.gough@gmail.com or via her Web site, www.orangepoppyjewelry.com.

Lauren Hadley is inspired by the contour, color, and texture of the unique materials she uses. View her work at her etsy shop Jewelry Creations by MarieMarie at mariemarie.etsy.com or contact her by e-mail at mariemarie103@aol.com.

Lacy Halliwell is currently a student and jewelry designer in San Francisco, Calif. Jewelry is her passion, as she was raised in a family of jewelers. Contact Lacy at shoelace0202@yahoo.com.

Monica Han is an award-winning mixed-media jewelry designer and teacher in Potomac, Md. Contact her via e-mail at mhan@dreambeads.biz.

Linda Hartung is the co-owner of Alacarte Clasps & WireLace® and designer, teacher, and CREATE YOUR STYLE with CRYSTALLIZED™ – Swarovski Elements Ambassador. Contact her via e-mail at linda@alacarteclasps.com, or visit her Web sites, wirelace.com and alacarteclasps.com.

Lindsay Hastings has been a designer for 12 years in Cincinnati, Ohio. Come see her at a local art show, or contact her at phoenixrisingdesigns@yahoo.com or phoenixbartender.etsy.com.

Christine Haynes is an Accredited Jewelry Professional (GIA) who sells her unique jewelry to private clients and on her Web site at fezelry.com. She can be reached via e-mail at jewelry@fezelry.com

Contact **Stacy Hillmer** in care of *BeadStyle* magazine.

Cathy Jakicic is the editor of *BeadStyle* magazine and the author of the book *Hip Handmade Memory Jewelry*. She has been creating jewelry for more than 15 years.

Armed with his mantra, "What are you gonna make today?" **Steven James** incorporates beads and jewelry making into home décor and everyday living. Visit his Web site, macaroniandglitter.com, or follow him at facebook.com/stevenjames.

Danish-born jewellery designer **Camilla Jørgensen** followed her passion for charity work and got her hands dirty in Africa, where she met and married a Canadian pilot. Inspired by friends, she now designs full-time in Montreal. Contact her via e-mail at info@micalla.com, or visit her Web site, micalla.com.

Eva Kapitany began making jewelry when, instead of prescribing medication, her doctor suggested she find a fun activity to ease her depression. Her husband saw her beading one day and told her, "Whatever you're doing, keep doing it, 'cause I've never seen you happier." Eva's been depression-free and designing jewelry ever since. Contact Eva in care of Kalmbach Books.

Susan Kennedy makes glass beads in her home studio in Pittsburgh, Pa. To see more of her work, visit her Web site at suebeads.com or contact her at sue@suebeads.com.

Jane Konkel is Associate Editor of *Bead-Style*. Contact her through the magazine.

Melissa J. Lee is an award-winning metal clay artist and jewelry designer. She can be contacted at melissa@melissajlee.com or via her Web site, www.melissajlee.com

Jill Lindl owns and operates her retail stores, Bead Basics, in Coon Rapids, Minn. Visit her Web site, bead-basics.com.

Jewelry designer **Monica Lueder** enjoys adding an elegant flair to her designs. Contact her via e-mail at mdesign@wi.rr.com.

Contact **Andrea Marshall** in care of Kalmbach Books.

Carol McKinney approaches the creation of jewelry using her knowledge of interior design. Contact Carol McKinney through her Web site, lemonleopard.com.

Irina Miech is an artist, teacher, and the author of *Metal Clay for Beaders*, *More Metal Clay for Beaders*, *Inventive Metal Clay*, *Beautiful Wire Jewelry for Beaders*, and *Metal Clay Rings*. She also oversees her retail bead supply business and classroom studio in Brookfield, Wis., Eclectica and The Bead Studio, where she teaches classes in jewelry marking. Contact Irina at Eclectica, 262-641-0910, or via e-mail at eclecticainfo@sbcglobal.net

Roxie Moede is a part-time designer, who just can't get enough of beading. She can be reached at littlrox@yahoo.com.

Observing the color combinations of people's clothing inspires **Jennifer Ortiz's** beading designs. Contact her at jenortiz794@yahoo.com.

Elizabeth Perez is a part-time jewelry artist who creates simple yet affordable jewelry in Norridge, Ill. She can be contacted at beadybombom@aol.com or via her Web site, www.BeadyBomBomCreations.com.

Polymer clay bead artist **Heather Powers** is the creative force behind Bead Cruise and the Art Bead Scene. Visit her Web site, humblebeads.com, for more information or to contact her.

Contact **Salena Safranski** in care of *BeadStyle* magazine.

Contact **Karla Schafer** in care of Kalmbach Books.

When **Katherine Schwartzenberger** is not working at her sister's bead store, Stony Creek Bead & Gallery, she enjoys creating jewelry using different mediums. Contact her at stonycreekbead@hotmail.com.

Brenda Schweder is the author of the books, *Junk to Jewelry* and *Vintage Redux*, both from Kalmbach Books. A frequent *BeadStyle* contributor, Brenda has been published in Kalmbach's magazines, pamphlets, and books. Read Brenda's blog at BrendaSchwederJewelry/blogspot.com.

Kim St. Jean is a full-time designer and instructor based from her bead store, Expressive Impressions, in Charlotte, N.C. She can be reached at kim@kimstjean.com, or through her Web site, kimstjean.com.

Sara Strauss was trained in jewelry design at the Fashion Institute of Technology in New York. Contact her via e-mail at bluestaro@hotmail.com, or visit her

Web sites, sgsjewelry.com and sgsjewelry.etsy.com.

Amy Thompson creates her modern and uniquely handmade items in Cincinnati, Ohio. Contact her via e-mail at jewelrybybutterfly@yahoo.com, or visit her Web site, www.butterflyjewelry.etsy.com.

Helene Tsigistras' jewelry has been featured in *BeadStyle* and *Bead&Button* magazines. She has also contributed designs to several books, including *Easy Birthstone Jewelry*. Contact her via e-mail at htsigistras@kalmbach.com.

Debbie Tuttle is a full-time jewelry artist who creates her one-of-a-kind vintage-inspired jewelry from treasured antiques. She lives in the historical town of Charlton, N.Y. Contact Debbie at bijouxcreations@hotmail.com or via her Web site, bijouxcreations.com.

Tamira Williams is a boho artist who creates her jewelry in Winter Garden, Fla. Contact her at raiynecharms@msn.com, or visit her Web site, www.etsy.raiynecharms.com.

Laura Crook Woodard is a part-time jewelry artist specializing in wire and resin work. She can be contacted at laura.crook.woodard@gmail.com or via her Web site, clementinagoods.etsy.com.

Jean Yates, of Westchester County, N.Y., enjoys creating beading tutorials and has recently written a jewelry design book titled *Links*. Her specialty is wirework integrating polymer and lampworked beads. Contact her at prettykittydogmoonjewelry.com, or visit her blog at prettykittydogmoonjewelry.blogspot.com.

Index